ВZCTПОИ45

OPERATIONS MANUAL

·CREDITS·

World War Cthulhu Architect: Dominic McDowall
Line Developer: Scott Dorward
Creative Directon: Dominic McDowall and Jon Hodgson
Art Director: Scott Purdy
Writing: Scott Dorward, Martin Dougherty and Ken Spencer
Cover Art: Jon Hodgson
Interior Art: Scott Purdy and Sam Manley
Graphic Design and Layout: Paul Bourne
Editing: Andrew Kenrick
Publisher: Dominic McDowall

Published by Cubicle 7 Entertainment Ltd
Suite D3 Unit 4 Gemini House, Hargreaves Road, Groundwell Industrial Estate, Swindon, SN25 5AZ, UK. Reg. no 6036414

Find out more about *World War Cthulhu: Cold War* and our other games at www.cubicle7.co.uk

Disclaimer
This book contains descriptions of real places, real events, and real people. These may not be presented accurately and with conformity to the real world nature of these places, people, and events and are described in terms of the folklore, myths, and legends about them, further reinterpreted through the lens of the Cthulhu Mythos.

No offence to anyone living or dead or to the inhabitants of any of these places is intended. Just as these stories have formed the basis for local folklore, so they are being used here as the basis around which to spin tales about the ancient horrors from the imagination of H. P. Lovecraft and those who have expanded upon his visions.

·CONTENTS·

·INTRODUCTION·

WELCOME TO SECTION 46

While few of you will find yourselves on battlefields or facing enemy fire, never forget that we are at war. Your duties as intelligence officers will regularly place you in danger. Many of the people you rely on for information and support will betray or kill you without a second thought. You will sometimes have to support madmen and terrorists while leaving the noble to die or suffer. The world has crept to the brink of nuclear annihilation more than once in living memory, and while our leaders sign arms limitation treaties, there are still enough weapons out there to kill us all a thousand times over. And these are the least of our worries.

As members of Section 46, you are part of an older, deadlier battle. Like the Cold War, it has no borders, no rules and, if we fail in our jobs, no survivors. As time and technology change the world, Our Other Enemy changes with it. Some grow bolder, hiding behind the masks of New Age religions and self-help groups. Others span the world in ways that were never possible before, taking advantage of the same advances in travel and communications as we do. Worse, the line between armed extremist group and cult grows ever more blurred, and when we are especially unlucky, the two worlds bleed into one another.

Either one of these battles may seem overwhelming. Together, they are almost beyond human comprehension. Many of you will give your lives, your sanity or your freedom to keep safe people who will never know your names. You will have to do terrible things that will slowly poison your minds as much as Our Other Enemy may. And you will often do all these things with no official support and no possibility of rescue or salvation if the worst happens.

We know what we ask of you, and we ask it because we know what you are made of. Through your sacrifices, you hold off unimaginable nightmares. This is a war humanity cannot afford to lose.

— N

USING THE OPERATIONS MANUAL

The bulk of this book is made up of techniques for tradecraft, surveillance, agent recruitment, combat and covert operations, designed to help members of Section 46 in their intelligence work as well as their more secret struggle against the Mythos. These are collated from the practices of the various intelligence agencies whose members work secretly within Section 46. They provide guidance for field officers, analysts, recruiters and anyone who may have to on occasion to get their hands dirty.

Throughout the book, you will find boxed text that explains how these techniques translate into new game mechanics for *Call of Cthulhu.* These boxes are addressed directly to the player or Keeper, and are marked with the following symbol:

Additionally, there are a number of special inserts from N and his field officers. While members of the intelligence services are given thorough training, there are special considerations that need to be kept in mind when dealing with the Mythos.

These additions are not meant to be shared outside Section 46 under any circumstances. The notes are addressed directly to the reader and can be identified by the following symbol:

Finally there is an appendix that details a number of the more unusual or specialist weapons of the period.

We hope that this manual helps your investigators in their struggles in the secretive and murky worlds of espionage and ancient inhuman evil. If they fail, God help us all…

CHAPTER ONE
COMMUNICATION AND DECEPTION

·COMMUNICATION· AND DECEPTION

The word 'espionage' essentially means 'discovering secrets', and is routinely used as short hand for all intelligence work. However, discovering secrets is only part of what intelligence agencies do. Much of the information gathered is not secret at all, though it may not be in plain sight. For example, a great deal of data can be gathered simply by observing traffic patterns, ships in harbours, shift changes at local factories, routine troop movements and other activity that are not 'secret', as such. Few nations will permit known spies to operate freely in their territory, however. Thus there is an element of secrecy and deception about our intentions, which allows us to then observe the mundane.

Other data can be obtained by reading local newspapers and listening to the radio news, although again this may not be accessible to those located in Western home countries. A great deal of what might be considered espionage is nothing more than careful observation of what a local citizen could see freely in his daily life, made possible by a carefully crafted cover story that allows the operative to be where the opposition would prefer they were not.

Secret information is rather harder to obtain, since it is concealed as a matter of course. Obtaining it requires the sort of skulduggery normally associated with espionage: breaking and entering, intercepting mail, stealing documents or recruiting informants by some means. However, there is a huge difference between obtaining secret information and discerning the enemy's secrets.

To be any use, information must be collated and analysed, but for this to happen it must first be transmitted to friendly analysts. Communication is vital to operations if they are to have any meaning, although it also provides an opportunity for the opposition to monitor our activities and expose our networks. Indeed, it could be argued that communication is what intelligence work is all about. We communicate our findings back to the analysts, we monitor and intercept the communications used by others… and we also use communication to deceive and confuse our opponents.

Deception can take many forms, not all of them deliberate. If the opposition genuinely believes something to be true and we obtain that information then we, too, can be deceived. There have been instances of our own false information coming back via hostile channels and being believed! Deception is also allied to ambiguity and information denial. That is to say, it is desirable to deny the opposition as much information as possible, even routine data, in order to give him less to work with in the long term. This is one reason for keeping foreign spies out of our territory even if all they see is the routine and mundane.

Ambiguity also serves our purposes by forcing the opposition to doubt his sources and to be unsure if he can trust the data he does obtain. If some of the information gathered by operatives is wrong or misleading, this has more than a local effect – it means that other data must be treated with suspicion. By way of example, if a potential

enemy suddenly starts moving military forces around and undertakes reconnaissance overflights of the border regions, this suggests that something is about to happen. However, if this occurs every few months as part of a 'routine exercise', raising local tensions but little else, then we cannot be sure that this occasion is any different.

Creating ambiguity and denying the enemy useful information are not, strictly speaking, the same thing as deceiving the enemy, although deception plays a part in (and is facilitated by) both. Deceptions vary considerably, from the direct lie told or the false passport, to the far subtler process of encouraging the opposition to deceive himself about our strengths and intentions. The most effective deception encourages the opposition to jump to logical (but incorrect) conclusions then corroborate or reinforce those same conclusions, rather than seeking to convince him outright. It is much easier to convince an enemy that he is right in conclusions he has already drawn than to make him change his mind.

Deception, as a rule, serves two primary purposes. By deflecting suspicion or convincing the enemy that a person or object is harmless we can prevent that person or object from coming to harm. This is termed 'protective deception'. By deceiving the enemy we can achieve a specific goal and further our mission or improve the general strategic situation. This is an 'active deception', and will usually require multiple avenues of deceptive activity to convince the opposition. Few intelligence operatives will believe information that is not corroborated elsewhere.

 Servants of Our Other Enemy are not the trusting kind. These are not simple shopkeepers and clerks you can bluff or bull your way past. They know things, and they know the world they move in. You can trust in two advantages when maintaining your cover against them. The world of the Enemy is not monolithic, it is divided and secretive and thus few know its true breadth and depth. Second, these fellows are degenerate and often mad, and although dangerous, an operative can play on both these factors to deceive and misdirect them. –N

 Desperate and deranged only begins to cover Our Other Enemy, and this desperation is the best tool you have against them. They are fanatics in the most literal sense; their capacity for rational thought has long since evaporated. They are cunning and resourceful, as are many animals. –Steuben

LIES, DAMNED LIES AND AMENDED TRUTHS

The most convincing liar is someone who believes they are telling the truth. The next best thing is to build a framework upon which to hang lies, then to reinforce that framework with as much truth as possible. The aim is for an operative to come as close as possible to convincing themselves that they are telling the truth, after which convincing someone else becomes a lot easier.

A person who is asked questions, even quite searching questions, about their life and their business in a given place will normally be able to give natural-sounding answers. They may be nervous, especially if confronted by aggressive questioning or if they have heard that bad things happen in police custody, but their answers will still sound natural and plausible if they are telling the truth.

In other words, an innocent person nervously telling the truth should still be able to convincingly answer how many brothers and sisters they have, where they went to school and how they came to be out late tonight. They will be able to furnish details of their occupation, workplace and daily life without much thought. They may not be able to recall offhand specific details such as the make of their employer's car – that is the sort of thing some people take note of and others do not – but they will be able to give an idea of its type and colour if they have seen it at all.

Someone who does not have a ready answer to simple questions will provoke additional questioning even if they are not suspected of outright lying. If caught unprepared, an operative may have to invent a story that explains why they are doing whatever it is has provoked the questioning. It is difficult to come up with something convincing off the cuff.

This is the place where lies can first collapse – before they are even told. If the subject of questioning is obviously trying to invent details when asked or cannot provide off-the-cuff answers to simple questions, then they are almost certainly making things up. The best way to avoid this is for an operative to have a rehearsed story ready and for them to be as familiar with it as with their real life story. Contradictions make lies easy to spot, and a badly prepared story may have many.

It is possible to avoid this first pitfall by having a well-rehearsed story ready for anyone who asks, but this is not the best option. It may sound too pat, for one thing, and there is a huge difference between delivering what amounts to a prepared speech and answering questions in a natural manner. A set of quick and simple answers might suffice to get past the most basic of questioning, but to be reasonably sure of success a different approach is needed.

The key is immersion. An operative should be thoroughly familiar with their cover story and reasons for being wherever they are likely to be questioned, and this goes far beyond knowing that their cover is a business courier for a firm of London-based lawyers. The operative must mentally create the firm's premises, employees and other details, and should be able to describe previous business trips or incidents of note. In short, when the operative has to lie about who he is and what he is doing, he should not be parroting a story learned by rote; he should be speaking from memory – albeit created, imaginary memories.

When combined with a cool nerve and a familiarity with telling lies gained in training (if it did not exist before) this ability to speak naturally as if from memory makes lies difficult to detect. An effective operative should have already learned to control 'liars tells', such as nervous glances away from the person being lied to, fidgeting or a tendency to blab out far too much detail. People telling the truth do not trot out their entire rehearsed story at the drop of a hat; they speak with familiarity, often making assumptions about what the listener knows.

Most liars give themselves away in the delivery of their story, long before anyone actually considers the words that were spoken. If a lie is well delivered, this can often be enough to satisfy questioning – especially if there is no real reason for suspicion. Indeed, it is possible to say very little but make it sound natural enough that the questioner lets the matter go.

If a lie gets past the delivery stage, then the lie itself must stand up to inspection. Few lies are more than three layers deep; that is, a questioner can usually find a hole in any given story with a couple of questions. For example, if an operative is posing as a university professor researching a book on the ancient history of the region then it stands to reason that he will be able to answer questions about who will publish the book, what other books he has written, which university he works for and so forth. He should also be able provide some information on the subject of the book – or at least he must be able to say something that sounds plausible.

Again, good preparation is essential to effective lying. If the delivery of the lie does not reveal it for what it is, and the fabrication does not collapse when questioned a little more deeply, then most questioners will be satisfied. If not, then they will have to work at disproving the lie, which is far more difficult than simply poking a hole in it and watching it unravel.

It is not always possible to thoroughly prepare a background and supporting information, so an operative should always have a framework in mind to hang the details on. Elements of the operative's own life can be used – these are likely to be both plausible and familiar – but this is not always appropriate to the situation. The key is to have a firm basis onto which details can be slotted at short notice, enabling the operative to build a cohesive story quickly if necessary.

The operative should always lie from a solid basis – and he must be aware that there is more to a lie than the information it contains. A lie should be delivered so that it sounds like it is coming from who the operative is pretending to be. A farm labourer will use different words and analogies to an oil company engineer; someone confident in his status or power will answer questions differently to a nervous citizen stopped in the street by the police.

Obviously, the lie must be consistent, and should contain just enough information to sound plausible. That is not the same as 'enough information to satisfy the questioner' – it may be that a plausible answer will be followed by more searching questions. This is how the game is played; the operative must resist the temptation to give the questioner all the information he could possibly want all at once, as this will seem suspicious in its own right.

The operative should know more than he is saying, and always be able to furnish more information, but should always remember that there are two stages to lying. The first is to convince the listener that the operative is not lying, and the second is to make him believe what the operative is saying is true. The closer a lie is to what the listener already believes to be true (which may not be the same as the actual truth!) then the more likely it is to be believed.

 One of the most important, and perhaps the most dangerous, lies you are going to tell is the one to your agency. The activities of our section must remain secret; the risk is too great if we are discovered. By piggybacking on another mission we gain access to greater resources than working on our own, but also expose ourselves. In a very real sense, your identity as an operative for your nation's agency is a cover, and one that must withstand even closer scrutiny than any you may adopt in the field. -N

BELIEVING YOUR OWN LIES

An investigator who wants to try to internalise their cover story enough that it no longer feels like a lie may attempt a Hard Intelligence roll to cement all the details. If successful, this will allow the player a bonus die on any rolls (usually social skills) made when defending details of the cover.

If the investigator is suffering from indefinite insanity, this can be a risky proposition. The Keeper should feel free to use the rules for delusions to project aspects of the cover identity into the investigator's life and vice versa, as they become less sure of which identity is the real one.

DISGUISES AND COVER IDENTITIES

Perhaps the most important lie an operative will tell is their cover story: the false identity they assume in order to go about their business. All of the principles of lying apply to the creation of a cover identity that will resist attempts to penetrate it.

A cover identity is different to a disguise, and different again to a cover story concocted for a particular mission. The latter is a plausible explanation for why an operative is in a given area, what they are doing and why they are not causing any kind of problem. Everything that operatives do in foreign territory (and most of the things they do on home soil too) should have a cover story attached to it. This story should match their cover identity or their disguise at the time.

If the operative's cover identity is an office worker in a shipping firm, then there are many missions that can be covered by their routine activities. However, it would be hard to explain why a petty bureaucrat was on a farm several miles from their base city – at least in the course of their normal duties.

If a suitable story can be created then this might prove acceptable; if not, then the operative should temporarily disguise themselves as something other than their normal cover identity – and this disguise should match the cover story for the operation.

An easy way to disguise oneself as a servant of Our Other Enemy is to simply not bathe or clean one's clothes. Often these servants are at least somewhat insane and care little for their personal grooming. This is especially true of low-level servants who do not have to face the scrutiny of the mundane world. While it is best to let the grime accrue naturally, necessity at times requires an operative to hastily muddy their appearance a bit. Keep in mind the filth will need to look a part of the image, not simply smudged on. -N

I have learned the hard way that bums have their own communities, and take violent exception to new people on their turf. It's easier to infiltrate a cartel of heroin smugglers than the local street sleepers.
– Miller

It cannot be stressed enough that any operation or mission must have a cover story attached to it, even if that cover is nothing more than normal day-to-day business appropriate to the operative's cover identity. Often a long-term cover identity will suggest plausible cover stories for missions; it is worth considering carefully which operatives to use for any given operation, since some will be more easily able to fit with the cover story than others.

A cover story is the ostensible reason for a given set of actions. Some parts of a mission (such as blowing something up or stealing documents) cannot be covered, but a good cover story at least gives the operative a plausible reason to be in the area. This does not apply only to the mission itself; an operative may be suddenly asked to account for why a member of their network was in a place they would not normally be several weeks or months after the event. A good cover story will allow this to be explained long after the fact – and the story will only be strengthened by a little difficulty in remembering or looking up the records of which employees were where on that day. It might seem suspicious if there was an explanation ready at hand for something that happened months ago.

Cover stories will usually tie in with the operatives' long-term cover identity, unless they are using some other temporary cover or disguise for a given mission. Disguises can be part of a cover identity but are usually short-term and don't need to be as detailed. It is often possible to adopt the most rudimentary disguise with success, especially if the operative looks like he belongs.

For example, an operative who wants to be mistaken for a truck driver might well get away with nothing more than adopting a general mode of dress and not making a mistake that might give him away as someone who has never driven a truck. Such a disguise might not stand up to close inspection but it is likely to be sufficient to drive a truck into an unsecured loading area, wandering around while the cargo is loaded, then driving out again.

 While it may get hectic in the field, keep in mind that you might need more than one cover identity, especially when dealing with Our Other Enemy. You might run into a bit of trouble with a cover identity that needs to both be a respected businessman and a crazed follower of Some Thing. Nothing can blow a mundane cover faster than being caught in a compromising situation while pursuing your alternate mission. -N

It is not usually necessary to create a full backstory for this imaginary truck driver. Using a disguise is mostly a matter of not standing out and attracting attention, and quite often there is nothing more to it than that. An operative disguised as a police officer might be able to walk into a crime scene, pick up evidence and walk off with it without being questioned at all.

However, a disguise should usually be accompanied by a basic cover story – where the truck has come from, which precinct the policeman just transferred from, and so forth. The act of preparing such a story often helps the operative get so convincingly into character that he is less likely to be questioned.

A long-term cover story, on the other hand, requires careful preparation. Clothing, luggage, personal effects and documentation must all match, and care must be taken to make items seem natural. Nothing interests a customs agent more than a case full of brand-new clothes, and it does not matter whether the operative is thought to be a smuggler or a spy – caught is caught.

All the aspects of a good lie (see pg. 8) must be applied to a cover story, and more. The operative must be able to describe his background, childhood, employment and present circumstances in a natural and not-obviously-rehearsed manner. Most of this information will never be asked for, but by preparing it the operative builds the basis for his lies. Assuming they are well delivered, they will seem plausible and will defeat the three-layer test.

A good cover identity is accompanied by habits of dress, mannerisms and figures of speech that support it. It is not usually appropriate for an operative to try to impersonate someone from a culture they know little about. It is possible that such mistakes will go unnoticed if onlookers are equally unfamiliar with such a culture, but this cannot be relied upon. Something as simple as a gesture or a figure of speech can give an operative away, or at least engender suspicion.

 Our Other Enemy sometimes has international reach. A cell in Detroit might have connections with one in Paris. This makes repeat use of a cover hard, but if you can come up with a cover that Detroit and Paris both trust, use it. Just be ready to burn that cover if, and when, it gets exposed. - Miller

Props and other supporting items are also critical to a good cover story. Someone who is travelling or working overseas may not have many personal items with them, but they will usually have some items from home. Those who have lived in an area for a long time will have accumulated various paraphernalia – the absence of such items can suggest that the operative does not consider the area to be home.

Of course, items in the home are unlikely to be exposed to scrutiny unless a search is conducted, but the cover identity should still be maintained at all times. The operative's living space should remind them of who they are for the duration of an assignment and must fit with their cover identity. It is possible that foreign intelligence personnel may gain access to an apartment, hotel room or wherever else the operative is living, and they should see nothing to arouse suspicion that the operative is anything other than their cover identity claims to be. It can cause considerable strain to live a false life in this manner, but it is part of the intelligence business. Some operatives take to it better than others. Some can only manage fairly short assignments before the strain begins to show; in such cases the operative must be withdrawn before they compromises the network. Others can live their false life for years with no ill effects.

As a rule, it is much easier to maintain a 'slightly false' cover than a completely alien one. In other words, if an operative comes from an educated background they will find it more comfortable – and therefore less stressful – to pose as a foreign national in the target country on business (living a lifestyle similar to his usual one at home) than to pretend to be an uneducated migrant worker living a completely different lifestyle to the one the operative is used to.

 All too often, Our Other Enemy is underestimated in their ability to blend in with the mundane world. Members of cells still need to eat, they need to sleep and they need to meet one another. The Boss tends to look down on servants of Our Other Enemy and assume them to be dangerous yet often incompetent. A cover or disguise that places one as a needed service provider, a repairman, waiter or even a taxi driver, allows an operative to get close to the target in a manner that is both covert and beneath suspicion. Who notices the bellboy? Who cares about the background of the telephone repairman? Who even talks to these people? – Rodriquez

Levels of Cover Identity

A cover identity can be assessed according to its strength, which is defined as the level of scrutiny it can resist. The lowest level is the 'polite fiction', in which the operative makes little attempt to pretend that he is not an intelligence officer and the local authorities ignore the fact that he is so long as the fiction is maintained and no overt acts are undertaken. This is part of the intelligence game; many nations will tolerate one another's spies so long as they are polite about it and do not cause trouble.

There is a limit to how much an operative with this weak a cover identity can achieve – which is one reason for tolerance – but such personnel are useful as a means of collecting low-level information. It might even be in the target country's interests to allow this to happen. A deception can be carried out by allowing the operative to witness whatever the host nation wants them to see, but more commonly a nation will want reports to be submitted showing that nothing untoward is happening.

The weakest true cover identity is one that will satisfy lax or unconcerned inspection, sometimes defined as the 'bored passport inspector'. A cover identity that does not arouse the suspicion of an ordinary public official (with no affiliation to the intelligence services and no reason to be alert) is good enough for many purposes, especially for a short mission. Such a cover can be thrown together quickly with little more than a briefing and some mental preparation, appropriate clothes and haircut, and documents that will usually include a passport.

A cover of this sort can be deepened later by adding more elements, but as a rule a light cover will be used for a single mission and then abandoned. It will not withstand even a moderate investigation, though it may take the opposition

some time to find the gaps in the story. Making a cover of this sort work is mainly about avoiding suspicion and not attracting attention. Once the operative is investigated, they will more than likely be found out.

 Maintain a forgettable and bland appearance, it makes it easier to become a cast off of society or a leader of the higher culture. Sadly, my appearance is far too distinctive for such measures. – Steuben

A strong cover is prepared in far more detail, and is necessary for a long-term deployment. The operative needs to have detailed knowledge of the cover identity's life and work, and there must be corroborating evidence. The operative's workplace and residence must comply with the cover identity to a degree that a detailed search – assuming it does not find anything incriminating such as a weapon or a false passport – will actually serve to strengthen the cover identity. If this level of cover is investigated by local intelligence services they should find only evidence that corroborates it.

The very strongest of covers is backed up by evidence 'back home'; in other words, if an enemy intelligence service sends investigators to the operative's ostensible home town they should find evidence that the operative lived there. If the operative claims former military service, there should be convincing records in the appropriate archives.

BONUSES AND PENALTIES ON COVER IDENTITIES

 As discussed, certain preparations or circumstances may strengthen or weaken an investigator's cover. The following list gives some ideas about when to apply bonus or penalty dice to rolls made defending an investigator's cover (usually social skills). There will always be special circumstances, and the Keeper should use this list as inspiration for eventualities not explicitly mentioned.

- The cover identity is not appropriate for the mission: 1 penalty die
- The cover identity is well-prepared and rehearsed, with suitable props and supporting documentation: 1 bonus die
- The cover identity has been improvised with little or no time to prepare: 1 penalty die
- The cover identity is similar to the investigator's own in nationality, education and social status: 1 bonus die
- The cover identity is utterly unlike the investigator's own in nationality, education and social status: 1 penalty die
- The cover identity is backed by details 'back home': 1 bonus die

It is probable that the opposition will never gain access to this information and that the effort put into it might seem to be wasted, but that is not so. First, it is always possible that our own intelligence services have been compromised, or that the opposition might somehow gain access to records – or a lack of them – that could expose the operative as a fraud.

Even if this is not the case, the fact that such careful preparation has gone into creating a cover identity will remove doubt from the mind of the operative. If he knows that the opposition cannot discover that he was never 'really' dishonourably discharged from the Royal Air Force – because there are records to show he was, and people who can remember it happening – then his confidence in his identity is strengthened. This can be a critical factor in surviving an investigation, since the weakest part of an operative's cover identity is of course the operative himself. Whatever props and supporting data may exist, one mistake on the part of the operative can reveal him for what he is.

INVESTIGATION, INTERROGATION AND TORTURE

Torture is an unreliable means of obtaining information, but that does not mean that a captured operative will not face it. Most intelligence services understand that information extracted under torture is useless, as the subject will usually say whatever the torturer wants them to. There are those that still think physical torture serves a useful purpose, however, and in fact it can. But that purpose is not obtaining reliable, accurate intelligence from an unwilling subject.

Torture or the threat of torture can be used to coerce someone into carrying out an act, either immediately or at a later date under threat of further punishment if they fail. Torture might be used to coerce an operative or someone associated with a network to steal documents or lead colleagues into a trap. It can also be used to weaken the subject's will, but used alone it rarely succeeds as a method of investigation.

The lower sorts of people can easily be intimidated or bribed into cooperation, and rarely have the necessary intellect to willingly serve Our Other Enemy. Some do so in a rote manner, much as many of the faithful do during their weekly services. These sorts should be your targets, they lack the ability to truly believe in what they espouse and yet are weak enough to be manipulated with ease. – Steuben

A subject might be beaten upon capture or afterwards, or tortured with a view to wearing down their will to resist, but this will be used alongside subtler methods of interrogation. Drugs are sometimes used to confuse the subject or to weaken their will but again, this does not always provide truthful, useful, or even coherent information.

The best way to obtain reliable information is to convince the subject that they want to give it to you or, failing that, to trick the subject into revealing it. One common gambit is to use physical violence as a demonstration of what might happen, then befriend the subject and 'protect' them from it, perhaps by making them believe that they have been transferred to a different and rather gentler set of captors. A combination of reducing the subject's faith in their peers and their loyalty to their country, the offer of rewards or at least freedom, and the building of a bond between interrogator and subject are all common ways to bring them from a position of determined defiance to one of willing compliance. This process can be subtle, and often involves asking the subject for something minor at first; once they begin complying they will generally continue to do so.

The measures used against a suspected operative will vary depending on how certain the captors are that the captive is an intelligence agent, and how much they think they can get away with. They may be prevented from going too far by their own people; for example, if the subject is being held in a police station, the enemy's intelligence services might not be willing to inflict violence even if they could get away with it, as they might not want to draw attention or cause a conflict with local law enforcement agencies. In some areas there are no such considerations and the operative is at the mercy of whoever has access to them.

Of course, this is the most extreme situation, with the operative in custody being interrogated whilst their place of residence is searched and their work colleagues questioned. For things to reach this stage, the situation must have progressed through several stages.

Stage 1: Routine Observation

The lowest level of threat to an operative's cover identity is that of routine observation by law enforcement personnel, enemy intelligence services who are not particularly alert or suspicious, and anyone else who might think there is something a bit off about the operative and take an interest.

Assuming the operative's appearance matches their cover story and they have basic documents, so long as they do not make any stupid mistakes they should not arouse undue suspicion. This level of threat to the operative's identity is constant and passive; there is always the chance of discovery, but it is unlikely and nobody is actively looking for them.

If the operative does attract attention, the most likely result is a fairly casual set of questions: a routine investigation, as described below.

Stage 2: Routine Investigation

A routine investigation takes place whenever someone questions the operative's cover identity in any way. This might be nothing more than a casual question from an

innocent stranger, or a requirement to present documents at a border crossing. Again, the questioner has no real reason to suspect the operative, but they are doing something that requires an answer and that answer will be evaluated.

A routine investigation of this sort might be unrelated to the operative's activities (border guards always ask for passports, not just when they think someone might be a foreign agent) or related (for example, when passing a police patrol after carrying out an act of sabotage that has raised alert levels). Either way, there is no direct suspicion; defeating this investigation is a matter of telling good, plausible lies whilst looking the part and having the right documents.

A routine investigation will usually take the form of a few questions and the presentation of documents. Questioners will not normally be seeking to catch the operative in a lie, but will likely spot a weak story and investigate further. If so, the investigation becomes an active investigation.

Stage 3: Active Investigation

An active investigation might be undertaken if the operative is caught doing something suspicious, or if evidence from elsewhere points to the operative. An error in dealing with a lower level of threat might also result in it escalating to an active investigation. The questioner now has good reason to suppose that the operative is hiding something, and wishes to find out what it is. Note that the questioner might not suspect the operative of being a spy; they may believe the operative is a criminal or be convinced they are hiding something but unsure as to what.

At Stage 1 and 2, it would normally be sufficient to leave the questioner in doubt that the operative is guilty of something; the default position is usually 'innocent until strongly suspected to be guilty'. At Stage 3 this position is reversed: the operative will have to make the questioner believe their innocence, and may have to do so despite a significant body of evidence or suspicion.

If dealing with police or other bodies bound by due process, it may be enough to not admit to anything or to obfuscate the issue to the point where it becomes clear a conviction will be impossible to achieve. However, in many parts of the world due process is unheard of, and some agencies will waive it if they have strong suspicions.

The operative will face persistent and repeated attempts to trap him in a lie or a contradiction, to ask questions that he would be able to answer if innocent but cannot, or to get him to admit to something. His workplace and abode will likely be searched, and he will be required to account for his movements. It may still be possible to defeat such an investigation by protesting innocence, providing good explanations and so forth, but the operative will need an airtight cover and a good performance under interrogation to succeed.

Stage 4: Hostile Interrogation

If the operative is believed to be such by their captors (or they believe the operative to be guilty of a serious enough crime) then they face an openly hostile interrogation – quite likely with no regard to the niceties of law. It is virtually impossible to defeat such an interrogation and be released having been found to be innocent; the best the operative can hope for is not to give too much away under interrogation and perhaps survive to be rescued or exchanged at a later date.

A hostile interrogation may or may not involve drugs and torture, but it will certainly be lengthy and unpleasant. In most cases, the interrogator will begin convinced that the operative's cover story is bogus or that they are guilty of a major crime, and will mainly be concerned with proving it or getting the operative to provide additional information.

A truly incredible performance coupled with an excellent cover identity might just be enough to let the operative beat the interrogators, but under most circumstances a hostile investigation will end only when the interrogators have some reason to conclude it. That could mean imprisoning or executing the operative, passing the operative to another agency or continuing to hold them indefinitely while they deal with other matters. At this point there is little the operative can do to save themselves; they can only hope that their release is somehow engineered – and that is both unlikely and out of their hands.

Defeating Investigation

Operatives must bear in mind that their cover identity is subject to challenge on a constant basis. Quite literally, every time they speak, interact with someone or are even just observed by a casual passer-by their cover identity can be 'blown'. This threat is constant and for the most part passive; if the operative has not aroused suspicion then the threat still exists, but nobody is actively trying to find holes in his cover.

Nevertheless, this routine threat can result in operatives being exposed. A chance word, a gesture out of place or some other minor slip up could cause someone to look more closely. It is countered, of course, by constantly remaining 'in character' and developing habits that support the cover identity.

Routine and trivial interactions with police and local officials – including non-government personnel such as railway staff, for example – also fall under the category of routine and passive threats. A border official glancing at passports or a policeman scanning the crowds on the alert for trouble will not specifically be trying to penetrate an operative's cover, but will notice anything out of place and investigate.

This level of threat requires no special measures from the operative. Their cover is already built; all they have to do is act natural and do what whoever their cover identity would do under the circumstances. A quite feeble cover or a simple disguise might well be sufficient, providing the operative gives the observer no reason to look more closely.

Degrees of alertness vary; it is always possible to encounter a minor official just after he has been reprimanded for laxness or a normally observant police officer who is tired at the end of a long shift. It may be possible to manipulate the situation in order to reduce alertness, such as passing a checkpoint at a very busy time or taking advantage of some distraction.

 Always keep in mind that Our Other Enemy possesses abilities above and beyond what one would expect from even the most sophisticated

technological surveillance. Through occult and esoteric means you might be spied upon, observed and even investigated, often without any clue to tip you off. Maintain your cover identities to greater depth and for greater lengths than you feel would be required for there is no safe place to let your guard down.
—N

None indeed. — Steuben

A common and effective gambit when leaving the scene of an operation is to join a crowd, fleeing with them if appropriate or gawking and dispersing. An operative who does not look out of place and who does what everyone else is doing is unlikely to be spotted, and providing there is no reason for this gambit to fail (such as being covered in blood or dishevelled from a fight) then it is far more effective than trying to slip away as everyone else is moving towards the scene of an incident. However, it does require a cool nerve to stay in proximity to an incident, and if onlookers are being questioned then remaining can be counterproductive.

Once someone takes an interest in the operative, things become a little harder. Active questioning of this sort might not be hostile; many questions are routine and do not indicate grave suspicion, merely that a situation has arisen

DEFEATING PASSIVE THREATS

The main skill used to stay in character and maintain a cover is Disguise, though there may be times when the Keeper decides to dispense with a skill roll — if the player does a good job of describing how suspicion is avoided, this can be rewarded by not having to roll the dice.

Defeating simple, passive threats to a cover is a very basic function for an undercover investigator, and under most circumstances they should be able to go about their business without blowing their cover. The Keeper might ask for a skill roll every few weeks of operations, but a failure does not necessarily mean that the investigator is blown. Sometimes people just fail to notice little things... or even quite big ones. However, knowing that a roll was failed a few weeks back might increase a player's paranoia — was the investigator 'made' and now being tailed? This sort of worry is an excellent way for the Keeper to torment players.

A skill roll is also needed (but can be dispensed with, as noted above) when the investigator encounters a threat to their cover, such as when crossing a border or interacting with officialdom. In this case the investigator must make a Disguise roll and, if successful, they need do nothing more — they have not aroused any form

of suspicion and, unless they have done something very stupid like trying to cross a border without a valid passport, they will be able to go about their business unhindered.

If the Disguise roll is failed, all is not lost. Errors might not be noticed by bored, tired or lax officials. The Keeper should make an opposed Spot Hidden roll to find out. This represents the whole process, even if the investigator has to present their passport and state their business multiple times. The skill level of the officials can be adjusted to suit their state of alert.

If the Spot Hidden roll is failed, the investigator's gaffe goes unnoticed. If it succeeds, the usual result is a round of more searching questions. See *Defeating Active Questioning*, opposite.

The investigator may try to explain away the gaffe using a social skill before the matter escalates enough for them to face active questioning. This qualifies as pushing the failed Disguise roll: if the player fails this pushed roll, the Keeper is at liberty to introduce further complications, such as the authorities inflicting a vicious beating as they detain the investigator, or the investigator inadvertently incriminating a colleague or agent.

in which the operative must be asked some questions and their answers evaluated. Previous comments about level of alert and distractions apply here, too.

However, once this situation has arisen the operative must actively defend their cover and explain their actions. They may well be asked the same questions as a 'passive'

DEFEATING ACTIVE QUESTIONING

Any active questioning faced by an investigator requires a higher level of skill to defeat than a simple trotting out of well-rehearsed answers to routine questions. Much depends on whether the questioning results from a routine requirement or whether there is real suspicion, but in all cases the investigator will have to account for their activities in a manner that is in keeping with their cover story. The Keeper might grant a bonus die or not require a skill roll at all if the player spins a good story, but in the case where the authorities are sure they have caught a spy there are limits to how much can be achieved by telling lies.

If the active questioning is fairly routine, there will be no serious attempt to poke holes in the investigator's story and certainly no violence. All that will happen is the questioner will be a little suspicious and will want plausible-sounding answers that satisfy their curiosity. Where the investigator is under serious suspicion or is subject to a hostile interrogation, the questioner will make determined efforts to find something wrong with the story.

In either case, the investigator must make a Fast Talk or Persuade roll to provide suitable answers that sound plausible. If this is routine questioning they will be released if their answers are acceptable and will probably not be under any more suspicion than before. Failing this roll means that the investigator will be detained and formally interrogated.

Note that 'interrogation' simply means rigorous questioning. There are circumstances where violence or harsh measures might be used but most interrogations do not involve physical coercion. They are, however,

a battle of wits and wills between the investigator and the interrogator.

This situation is important enough to be role-played in some detail. The interrogation process is exhausting for the investigator, even if there is no physical coercion. They must pass an CON roll, or else their will breaks and they admit something that compromises them. Assuming this is passed, the interrogation takes one or more 'rounds'. During each round the investigator must make a Persuade or Fast Talk roll to plausibly answer questions, with the difficulty level set by the the interrogator's Psychology skill.

- If the investigator succeeds and the interrogator fails, the interrogator buys their story and releases them.
- If the investigator fails, the interrogator becomes sufficiently convinced that the investigator is lying to hold them. They will be passed to the appropriate authorities, depending on what the interrogator believes the investigator is guilty of.
- If both succeed or both fail, the battle of wits continues.

If the interrogator uses torture, the CON roll can be made Hard or even Extreme depending on the Keeper's decision about the severity of the torture. However, if torture is used then so long as the investigator succeeds in their Fast Talk or Persuade roll, the interrogator will probably decide that since they are sticking to their story despite torture, it may well be true. Release is likely at this point but the Keeper should decide whether or not the authorities still have suspicions about the investigator. This may lead to them being watched in the future.

investigation might ask – name, occupation, business in the area and so forth – but the questioner will be looking for holes in their story. The operative will likely be expected to furnish details and repeat them correctly. The questioner may quote back what the operative has said incorrectly to see how they respond, and in general will try to trip the operative up and catch them in a lie.

Providing the operative has a decent cover story and keeps their cool, this sort of active questioning can be defeated without extreme measures. In other words, the operative should be able to convince the questioner that they really are an innocent person going about legitimate business. The difficulty of doing this can vary considerably depending on who the operative is dealing with and their level of alert, but active questioning does not indicate that the operative is blown.

An operative will have to defeat at least routine active questioning numerous times in the course of a deployment. There is always a risk, but it is not usually significant unless the operative is caught doing something that is difficult to explain. However, the operative must observe the questioner carefully, as well as any associates they might have. If it seems that things are going awry, there may be an opportunity for escape. Naturally, someone who runs when questioned will be assumed guilty – of something at least – if caught, but a timely escape may be the best option if the interrogation starts to go badly.

A hostile interrogation is unlikely to take place in the street; the subject will almost always be detained and confined in some manner. This might be immediate, such as taking the subject to an interrogation room at a border post for further questioning, or the subject may be fully secured at a police station or a similar facility before interrogation. The latter suggests that the opposition are pretty sure the subject is guilty and are seeking confirmation or hoping to extract information; the former indicates a slightly lower level of suspicion.

The operative needs to weigh the odds and decide whether to try to bluff their way through the interrogation. Fleeing or attempting to shoot their way out might be the only option, but these are desperate measures that, even if successful, will have repercussions for the whole network.

It may be possible to use other methods to bypass the interrogation, such as bribery or threats of intervention by powerful friends. This can work, especially in corrupt regions or where the officials are unsupervised. A measure of deception is usually necessary when offering a bribe:

few officials will take money to let a foreign spy into the country; there is simply too great a risk of repercussions. However, the same official might well take a bribe to ignore minor discrepancies in paperwork when accompanied by a believable tale of administrative errors from an apparently harmless person.

Interrogators often claim or insinuate that they have proof of guilt, or that others will sell the subject out, and it is therefore in his best interests to make a deal and come clean. This is sometimes true but more commonly it is a gambit to trigger a confession. The operative might be able to figure out whether such claims are true by carefully observing the questioner – an interrogation can be a two-way process.

PROPS – FORGED, FAKED AND REAL

A cover identity requires a number of props; physical items that support and reinforce the cover. For a simple disguise, it is often possible to get away with using the most rudimentary of props; if a disguise will not survive close inspection due to its hasty nature, it matters very little whether or not the operative's shoes are authentic and convincing when carefully examined.

A different situation exists with a cover identity. Obviously, all items and clothing should look the part when subject to a casual glance from a distance. Greater authenticity provides defence against closer inspection. For example, a jacket might look fine from a distance but use a weave of cloth not normally seen in the operative's region. If anyone notices this, the operative will have to explain why they have an imported jacket. Foreign intelligence services will take a strong interest in someone who has clothing from a potential enemy nation, especially in countries where imports are not permitted.

The same goes for labels, methods of stitching and so forth. These will not be obvious to a casual glance, and even when answering a few routine extra questions at a customs post it is unlikely that officials will examine the label inside an operative's shirt collar. However, if they come under suspicion the operative might be closely examined, and such small details will confirm that the operative is a fake. At that point, their fate is sealed.

Props must therefore be as authentic as possible. If the operative is posing as a foreign businessman, they will of course have clothing from their own country. If they are pretending to be a local, they will not. It is often possible

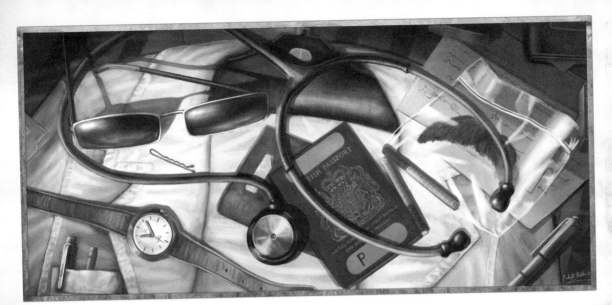

– and generally desirable – to obtain real items such as clothing, shoes, pens, handkerchiefs and such like once established in the target area, and to dispose of faked items as much as possible.

Some items are more difficult to obtain locally. Documents, passports and similar must be forged – and forged well. Care must be taken to correctly match paper types, bindings and embossing styles as well as the more obvious words and photographs. This can be done by our own intelligence services, but obviously takes time. Documents must then be brought to the operatives in the field, which can be a hazardous undertaking.

Forgers working in the criminal world can be a useful asset, and many countries have a thriving black market in documents including passports. This often occurs as a result of corruption, incompetence and inequality in a society. If ordinary people cannot obtain documents they need and are entitled to, forgeries may be the only solution. We can take advantage of this situation, although obviously any interaction with criminal elements can be risky in itself.

 Agents have at their disposal a selection of false documents relating to Our Other Enemy. These include forged diaries, grimoires and ritual instructions that are patently useless but appear to be genuine. Keeping abreast of new technologies, these are available in physical form as well as on microfiche and as photostat copies. These forgeries are expensive and dangerous to make, their use should only be as needed and not when other means of building a cover as cattle, an esoteric bookseller or other such person can be accomplished through other means. -N

 The last thing one would want to do is lose one of these excellent forgeries. However, one can take some solace in the fact that if lost they do not contain anything dangerous to the general public. -Steuben

Clothing and everyday items can be used to conceal or disguise necessary pieces of equipment, but wherever possible it is better to operate without a piece of equipment than to carry it just in case. Weapons, in particular, are highly incriminating if the operative is caught with them and should be carried only when an operational requirement exists. Some operatives like to have a weapon 'just in case', and this can boost confidence. This is a dangerous and amateurish attitude.

Weapons are hard to conceal. Even quite a small handgun is a bulky and solid object to conceal, and there are only so many places about the body one can be carried. A weapon will be found by even the most cursory of searches.

That said, if a weapon is needed then it can be concealed by clothing: waistbands and shoulder holsters can be covered by a jacket or a loose shirt, while ankle holsters can be concealed by trouser legs. Most people will not notice a weapon even if it causes a slight bulge in clothing, and sometimes even a weapon held in the hand can be concealed by keeping the hand below the waist and close to or behind the leg.

This may seem overly simple but it is possible to walk right up to someone with a handgun or a knife held in this manner, perhaps keeping their attention with the other hand, and still deliver an attack by complete surprise. However, bodyguards and law enforcement officers are trained to look at a subject's hands and will spot a gun or knife carried in this way.

Weapons can be concealed in other objects, perhaps in a disassembled condition. The decision of when to put the gun together must be finely judged, especially in a time-critical scenario. A weapon simply put in a bag and concealed by other items will be spotted as such by a search, whereas a disassembled weapon might be disguised as a collection of harmless items.

Other equipment can also be concealed or disguised, though it must be reiterated that any piece of 'spy equipment' can be incriminating; the less an operative is carrying, the smaller the chance of discovery. One of the commonest pieces of equipment is a device for concealing other small items. A brooch, cufflinks or the heel of a shoe can be hollow and used to carry a range of small items. Similarly an attaché case or other bag can have concealed compartments. The lining of a coat or jacket offers other possibilities for concealment.

Of course, all of these measures are well known to the intelligence services of most countries and are therefore not guaranteed to evade detection by a proper search. If possible, items should be disguised in novel ways or not carried at all; what is not there cannot be found no matter how thorough the search may be.

COMMUNICATIONS

To be of any use, information must be transmitted to the end user, whether orders and instructions, requests for support or equipment, or intelligence gathered through an operation. We can disrupt or intercept the communications of others, and in turn they can do the same to us. Communications is a field where the sword has two edges: we must be on our guard for measures that we ourselves are using elsewhere.

Radio and telephone communications offer a fast and reliable means of passing information, but can be intercepted or eavesdropped. As a rule, operatives should not say anything on the telephone that they cannot explain away under their cover story. There are simply too many ways for the opposition to eavesdrop, and even just knowing that the operative made a call to a certain number can be enough to trigger an investigation.

Much the same apply to radio communications. Very few people use radio in their daily lives, so unless the operative's cover includes an interest in 'ham' radio (by itself potentially arousing suspicion that would otherwise not exist) they will have no good explanation for being caught with a radio.

Radio communications, if used at all, should never be 'in clear' (in other words, not encoded in some way) and should be carried out from a remote area where discovery is unlikely. Many intelligence and law enforcement agencies routinely scan for unlicensed radio broadcasts including pirate radio stations and other non-espionage uses, and can use direction-finding equipment to locate a transmission site.

If radio is to be used then it must be assumed that a transmission will be intercepted at some point, and that the authorities will attempt to find the transmitter. The only way to avoid this is to keep moving it and to make essential broadcasts only. These should be as short as possible and encoded in some manner.

The alternative is to use a transmitter that the opposition cannot shut down, and to get the content for broadcasts to it covertly. If secret information can be hidden 'in plain sight' among innocent content, it may be possible to use a civilian transmitter or a pirate radio station to communicate. Similarly, radio broadcasts of an innocuous nature can be used to convey information or instructions by means of prearranged codes. This form of radio communication is limited but less risky than a lengthy two-way conversation.

The interception of radio-frequency signals forms part of the Electronic Intelligence (ELINT) and Signals Intelligence (SIGIT) fields. This is typically beyond the remit of most field operatives, who specialise in traditional 'human intelligence' (HUMINT), but may at times be relevant.

Our Other Enemy rarely makes direct use of anything that can be picked up with SIGIT or ELINT. More likely, their activities will impact local communications systems. Strange whispers or even shadowy images can be sure signs of the presence of Enemies from other realms. Standard SIGIT or ELINT protocols can be used to narrow down a location or investigate and anomaly. -N

ELINT operations seek to obtain useful information from any and all transmissions made by the enemy. Much can be learned from the fact that a radio transmitter is broadcasting from a certain place, or that a radar set has been used in a particular locality. Analysis of the transmission can indicate what type of radar or radio is in use, which in turn allows conclusions to be drawn about the type of installation or activity it is used for.

For example, maritime navigational radar has a different signature to air defence radar, and radars associated with short-range anti-aircraft guns or missiles are different from those used to detect high-flying bombers or to guide long-range air defence missiles. Thus, by monitoring transmissions from a site our analysts can determine that a major strategic air defence installation is in the area. It may be more difficult for them to obtain photographs of the installation or to steal documents from it – which is where HUMINT becomes critical.

 Sometimes you have to look in the spaces between spaces, so to speak; or at least the signals between signals. Just don't let them look back. - Miller

SIGINT seeks to obtain information from the opposition's transmissions. This requires the interception and decryption of transmissions, which can be a lengthy and difficult process. Much can be learned from callsigns and the fact that radios were in use at a particular time, and if signals can be fully decrypted this can yield a treasure trove of information. HUMINT plays a part in obtaining the means to decrypt transmissions: code books and the like are high-value targets, and it is possible to achieve much by simply learning the opposition's radio procedures.

 Listening in on Our Other Enemy and their freak impacts on SIGIT and ELINT is very dangerous, despite the value the Boss places on such techniques. It is far too easy to hear something that you shouldn't while straining to hear something that you need to. If you think not being able to get a disco number out of your head is bad, try that with one from Elsewhere. - Rodriguez

Naturally, all of these measures can be used against us as readily as by us. For this reason, most communications within a network should be direct and personal. Documents, photographs and reports will normally need to be physically handed between operatives and taken to a location from where they can be sent or transmitted home. Once items reach friendly territory or a place from where they can be carried in a diplomatic bag (which, by treaty, is immune to inspection) then it is reasonably certain that they will reach the destination. However, diplomatic bags are sometimes snatched and other 'secure' communications can still be compromised.

Radio and telephone communications should only be used for very urgent messages or where no other alternatives exist. The shorter the message and the less overall time spent on the air, the smaller the chance of interception. One way to achieve this is to use code words and phrases. These can convey important information in a very short space of time.

To make it difficult to infer a meaning to a code, words and phrases should be assigned randomly to a preselected list of meanings. A set of phrases will normally include a 'duress code', which permits the operative to warn listeners that something is badly wrong – normally this means they are being forced to make the transmission.

 We inherited a set of codes from our wartime predecessors, and even though our intelligence services are known to have been penetrated by the opposition these have, for the most part, not been changed. The one-word codes assigned to Mythos creatures by Network N during World War Two are still in use.

These codes are contained in document 'Case Seven'. They are on the Reserved List and are never assigned as reporting codes by the Western Allies. The Reserved List contains numerous special-case codes, most of which fall outside our remit and their meanings are therefore, quite rightly, not available to us. Only those assigned a set of Reserved Codes are to know of the list's existence, and revealing that we know of the list will indicate to outsiders that we are involved with at least one of the Special Cases. We do not want the attention this may bring about.

All references to Our Other Enemy - in all forms of communication - must be encrypted and should use Case Seven reporting codes rather than the actual names of creatures. The opposition must not suspect that we have agents abroad with knowledge of unusual activity and creatures. Our task will become enormously more hazardous if our personnel are hunted for their knowledge and their transmissions become a signal for enemy investigators to descend upon an area. -N

CASE SEVEN CODE WORDS

★ ★ ★ ★ M O S T   S E C R E T ★ ★ ★ ★

To avoid revealing information about Our Other Enemy to telegraph and radio operators, the following code words should be used in all written and transmitted communications. If no codeword can be found for an event, use the nearest approximation and prefix with COLD.

Burn this document as soon as you have memorised it.

SUPPER: Occult Text, Class One (e.g. *Necronomicon, De Vermis Mysteriis*).

TIFFIN: Occult Text, Class Two (e.g. *Saracenic Rituals, The People of the Monolith*).

LEFTOVERS: Occult Text, Class Three (notes, diaries, etc.).

PITCHFORK: Dagger, Ritual.

HAYSTACK: Altar, Sacrificial.

PIGSTY: Suspected Summoning Site.

ABATOIR: Confirmed Summoning Site.

CATTLE: Cult, Malignant.

SCARECROW: Sorcerer, Lone.

CARBUNCLE: Portal to non-terrestrial destination.

BUNION: Subterranean temple or catacombs.

POLONIUS: Ghoul.

COLD POLONIUS: Subterranean creature of unknown classification.

OPHELIA: Deep one.

COLD OPHELIA: Aquatic or amphibious creature of unknown classification.

NETWORK N
EYES ONLY

HANDLING RADIO COMMUNICATIONS

The basics of using a radio transmitter are taught to all field operatives, along with standard measures for avoiding detection. Investigators can be assumed to be able to set up a fairly standard transmitter or send a signal on the desired channel. Other operations require the use of the investigator's skills in a slightly unusual context.

Attempting to avoid detection involves a combined Signals and Tradecraft roll. A successful roll will usually indicate that the transmission was sufficiently short and well-timed to avoid detection by routine measures.

Any task that requires modifications to the set, significant adjustments to overcome local conditions or repairs, uses Electrical Repair skill. For example, modifying a set to broadcast on an unusual channel or to burn through interference would use this skill.

Most other operations are simply applications of what the investigator has been taught about radio communications, falling under the Signals skill. Fairly simple tasks will be completed with ease; more complex or unusual applications can be covered by a skill roll.

Signals, Codes and Ciphers

A code essentially substitutes a word, symbol or phrase for a piece of information. This may be a particular subject such as a place, circumstance or person or a word or phrase. The use of a code will usually shorten a transmission by allowing the meaning of a message to be conveyed with a short phrase or a single word.

One-word codes convey a meaning rather than the specifics of the message. A prearranged code such as "Anchor" might mean something quite complex, such as the fact that a specific place has evidence of activity by Soviet intelligence agents but there are no signs of combat personnel there. The more specific a code is, the less generally useful it will be; most codes can be used to construct complex messages as they have a more general meaning, but very important pieces of information are usually assigned a specific code.

For example, the Soviet Northern Fleet might be given the code word "Brimstone" and the concept of "at sea, probably on exercise" be assigned the code "Roundabout". The phrase "Elements Brimstone Roundabout" indicates that at least part of the Northern Fleet has sailed from its home port on what is thought to be an exercise. It is unlikely that anyone without knowledge of the appropriate codes could deduce the meaning of this message even if they decrypted it.

Signals of various other sorts can also be used to convey a meaning. Prearranged signals such as a particular book on a windowsill can be used to indicate that it is safe for the operative to come to his informant's house, or that a message has been left at a prearranged drop point. Signals of this sort, like codes, require prearrangement and cannot convey a meaning that lies outside their field of coverage.

Ciphers, on the other hand, translate not the meaning of a word but its letters. This allows a message to be created with any meaning the Agent wants it to have, and then encrypted to make it hard to read. The problem with ciphers is that they can be broken by various means. If the 'key' to a cipher is known (such as from a captured enemy code book) then it can be read as easily as a clear transmission, but even if it is not known the cipher can sometimes be cracked by looking for common words.

As a result, a simple substitution cipher is of little value. Complex ciphers, which rearrange the letters in a word and break the text into blocks of a set length (such as four-letter blocks) can make it hard to recognise words, and of course mixing codes and ciphers results in a translation both of meaning and of actual text.

The most secure cipher likely to be available to an operative in the field is the one-use pad. This contains a key that can be used to encrypt any message, and is extremely difficult (perhaps impossible) to decrypt without the identical corresponding pad. Such pads allow communication only between an operative and the holder of the other pad and may thus suffer from some lack of flexibility. However, so long as proper channels for information flow have been set up this is an extremely secure means of communication.

HANDLING CODES AND CIPHERS

For the most part, use of codes and ciphers is routine; it is something all intelligence operatives are trained to do. Personnel will be able to automatically encrypt and decrypt their own messages and those using a system they have the key to. However, when an investigator wants to figure out a coded or ciphered message they have found, they will have a more difficult time.

A simple code can sometimes be broken with no outside help. Codes of this type are likely to be in use with amateurish dissident groups or possibly very backward national armed forces. An INT roll (or a Cryptography skill roll, if this is higher) will allow an investigator to decode a message encoded in a simple cypher). If they make a Hard success, they have broken the code and can read future messages that are sent using it fairly easily, though they will require some time to decode them. More complex codes, such as those used by the Soviet armed forces, cannot generally be broken by local means, if they can be broken at all. Decryption and analysis will usually have to be carried out by experts back home. Information gained from such complex codes will tend to be a matter of plot, not skill rolls. Operatives may sometimes be able to get a decrypt of an enemy code, but often will not. They may also be provided with information that has come in from other parts of the intelligence community such as decryption by SIGINT personnel or other, more secret, means.

DROPS AND OTHER FORMS OF COMMUNICATION

Some messages or information can be conveyed by a simple signal. The most common use for this is to inform members of a network that there is a message waiting in a dead drop. This system is used to build cut-outs into the communication system and protect operatives if some part of their network is compromised.

Thus an operative who spots a particular signal – say, a hat left on the dashboard of a certain car – knows that a given circumstance has occurred. The amount of information that can be conveyed in this manner is limited, but nonetheless can prove important. Prearranged signals of this kind are passive in nature and are unlikely to be detected, but equally the operative cannot be sure they will not be accidentally removed or simply not spotted by the intended recipient.

It is important to know the symbols the servants of Our Other Enemy use. Being obsessed creatures, they tend to use the same symbols over and over, and through this inattentively label their dead drops and other resources. That is not to say that every three lobed star is a sign that our friends who follow it are using a loose brick to pass information, but it is a viable clue. Still, more than one cell of cattle has been sent to slaughter through these means. –N

The initial signal conveys relatively little information, but if the message is "under observation, stay away" then this can be

invaluable. It can also inform the operative that more detailed information is available from a drop. The usual form of a drop message is written, probably coded or encrypted. A drop system can take the form of a verbal message left with a 'human drop' who knows only the message itself, not what it means. When given the correct identification phrase the human drop passes on the message and then goes on with their business.

Human drops have advantages and disadvantages. They allow communication between people who will never meet; but they add an extra person to the chain, which can increase the chances of detection. However, written messages have their own drawbacks.

Any written message can expose everyone involved to the risk of exposure if it is found, and can be used as evidence by the enemy more effectively than a verbal message might be. Written messages should thus be destroyed once they are delivered, ideally by burning.

While it may be all well and good for our esteemed spider to sit in his web and learn these things, those of us in the field must keep a certain detachment from the more dangerous and esoteric of our intelligence work. Failure to do so will lead the weak-willed to a dark end. – Steuben

In extreme circumstances, an operative may have to attempt a brush pass. This requires the operative to walk past the agent with whom them are exchanging information, making contact fleetingly to pass a message or item. If this is performed successfully, an observer will only see two people walking past

each other. The fact that the operative and their agent are in the same place at the same time is risky, however, and may raise suspicions even if the exchange goes unobserved. This technique should only be used when there is no other option.

Written messages can be concealed within an innocuous letter or card, either written in a 'secret ink' that only becomes visible when treated correctly or encoded within the text. Such a concealed message must be well enough hidden to evade at least casual notice. If there is any danger that the operative is under suspicion and their mail is being read, it must be very well concealed indeed. As with other written forms of communication, a letter with a secret component is all the proof that hostile intelligence personnel need.

Use of Propaganda and Lies

Propaganda takes various forms, some crude and some subtle. Certain regimes simply repeat the party line over and over through every medium possible until people believe the message even though they are fairly sure it isn't true. As a rule, the truth is a more powerful propaganda weapon than lies – not least since it is impossible to be caught in a lie if you have told the truth.

When working with local assets, truthfulness builds trust, though it may be necessary to balance truthfulness against the intended result – there are times when it is necessary to misrepresent a situation in order to make it look less disastrous. Operatives should be aware that being discovered to have lied may cause trust and cooperation to break down.

When a piece of propaganda makes no attempt to hide its origins, this is termed 'white propaganda'. Since the source is obvious, it is usually counterproductive to tell lies, but the truth can be told in a way that suits our purposes. We might, for example, put out the entirely truthful story that a recent Warsaw Pact military exercise was in fact staged and scripted, and its immense success was certain from the start. We might not mention the sheer size of the exercise and the numbers of tanks and aircraft involved, as we do not want to play up the strength of the enemy's forces.

White propaganda often consists of information the enemy would prefer not be made public, but which is true and can therefore be independently verified. White propaganda also serves our cause more indirectly; it will strengthen the reputation of our operatives for telling the truth when it is corroborated.

White propaganda also includes images and information that are not directly damaging to the enemy but which aid the friendly cause. For example, posters exhorting workers to meet their production targets or to foster goodwill towards allies. Neither are not directly harmful to the enemy, but it is designed to manipulate the populace into thinking in a way that the propagandists approve of. White propaganda is generally candid about its origins; for example pro-government posters will generally not conceal the fact that they were issued by the government itself.

Black propaganda is deliberately misleading about its origins. Often it will purport to originate from the enemy, such as fake radio broadcasts pretending to be foreign stations or 'leaked' documents revealing 'facts' that are damaging to the enemy. Black propaganda may be true or contain truthful elements, but more commonly is made up of lies.

You want to talk about black propaganda? It doesn't get any blacker than some of the books our other enemy pass around. They promise power, or at least safety, if you worship their damnable gods and make the right sacrifices. That's as pathetic as cows in a slaughterhouse praying to the man with the big knife. – Steuben

Somewhere between white and black propaganda lies the field of grey propaganda. Grey propaganda does not identify its source, or is vague about it, but does not deliberately attempt to mislead its origins. Often this is done to conceal whose agenda the propaganda supports. Grey propaganda tends to appear neutral in its viewpoint or to have been put out by legitimate bodies or persons.

For example, a fabricated report ostensibly published by a respected academic at a university with no political connections, but which is biased towards a particular viewpoint, might be considered a piece of grey propaganda. It would be 'black' if it purported to be sanctioned by a political body other than the one actually issuing it, but since it claims a neutral source it should be considered to be 'grey'.

The truth is a powerful propaganda weapon, and is more commonly employed in white than black or grey propaganda. However, all three types can make liberal use of truths, half-truths, deceptive statements and outright fabrication.

"Speak loudly and repeat" is the crudest form of propaganda. This technique is commonly used to indoctrinate a domestic population or to try to wear down the morale of enemies. There may be a few true details here and there to strengthen the story, but this sort of propaganda is for the most part simply made up to suit the purposes of the user. This can be very effective, especially when the local population has no other source of news than the official radio and TV channels or where it takes an indirect form.

Other forms of propaganda are subtler, and revolve around concealing some truths and using others in a misleading manner. For example, a prominent exponent of free speech and governmental reform might be arrested on a trumped-up charge (usually something nasty to appal the general population) and much made of the event. With no real case against him, he will eventually be released, but this part of the story might be suppressed. Although the mud thrown at this person's reputation is entirely invented, some of it will stick and his credibility will be damaged even though he is entirely innocent. This sort of propaganda relies on the spreading of rumours and gossip, and reporting through newspapers and radio.

 I'm not sure the boss would like this too much, but I've had some success in pitting groups of cattle against each other. Sometimes all it takes is the right words in the right ears, or a few planted documents. The next thing you know, they're playing "my god can beat up your god" and stabbing each other with sacrificial knives. — Rodriguez

 You are correct. I do not like this. These people have no concept of subtlety, and their petty battles risk exposing us all. —N

Propaganda often uses the truth in a manner that can be misleading, for example presenting unrelated events (that really did happen) as a conspiracy or master plan. A crashed spy plane, which came down due to mechanical failure, might be presented as shot down in the hopes of making the enemy believe the propagandists' side has weapons capable of engaging high-flying aircraft.

Propaganda of all types can be used to shape attitudes to various groups, for example fostering the belief that everyone of a particular nationality or ethnicity is corrupt or stupid. It can be used to destroy the reputation of a person or to shift the blame for a defeat, setback or unpopular decision on to a suitable scapegoat. Similar methods have been used to destroy former national heroes in many totalitarian nations strengthening the current regime.

Most operatives will use propaganda on a very local basis, such as presenting information in such a way as to win over local supporters.

A large-scale propaganda campaign intended to inspire local workers into a campaign of passive resistance or to stir up anti-government feeling is more likely to be orchestrated at home, with operatives in the field carrying out various tasks to facilitate it or make use of it.

 It is tempting to use propaganda against Our Other Enemy. The right words, especially in a country with a national religion or a strongly religious population, can turn official attention towards the cattle. You might even summon the spectre of populist mob violence. Such a scheme is all too prone to expose things best left occluded and rend the penumbra we work within. —N

The op went bust, but I legged it to safety, and with the parcel as well. This is how things can go wrong: you trust the wrong people. How was I supposed to know the Russian was 46 as well? If she was. Which she wasn't, wasn't. Back to Blighty for the debrief with the Guv. — Stanton

CHAPTER TWO

NETWORKS AND ASSETS

·NETWORKS AND ASSETS·

It is rare for an operative to work entirely alone. In order to carry out effective intelligence work it is necessary to build a network. This is always a risky business; each additional member of a network increases the chance of it being penetrated or revealed to the enemy, and bringing in a new asset always creates a period of increased risk. Some components of a network will be fellow intelligence operatives who can (usually) be trusted to be both competent and discreet. However, any intelligence agency can be compromised so. Similarly, some operatives are cowboys who take unnecessary risks or disregard procedures, while others are simply inept. A degree of mistrust towards everyone can be a boon among operatives, but too much of it can cripple an operation.

If fellow operatives are subject to slight mistrust (or at least, not being above suspicion when something goes wrong) then local assets are not to be trusted at all. An asset is someone who carries out some task for the network, either regularly or as needed. A good network has many assets, run by one or more case officers, but can disconnect itself from any or all of them at need.

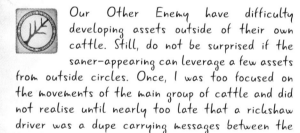

Our Other Enemy have difficulty developing assets outside of their own cattle. Still, do not be surprised if the saner-appearing can leverage a few assets from outside circles. Once, I was too focused on the movements of the main group of cattle and did not realise until nearly too late that a rickshaw driver was a dupe carrying messages between the two leaders. – Rodriquez

Yes, Our Other Enemy uses much the same methods as we do. In turn, we must use those methods to a higher degree of efficiency. The stress this entails means that you may have to use and cast off assets often. If a few healthy cells must be cut out to excise the cancer, then so be it. – Steuben

Operatives with jobs within the network need access to a certain amount of information, though this can be compartmentalised to prevent any one person revealing too much. Assets do not need much information at all, though they may require some to be able to function or to secure their loyalty. Assets should never be trusted with mission-critical information or secrets that could compromise the network as a whole.

Note that one of the greatest dangers to an intelligence network is a shift in the loyalties of its own people. An operative might be compromised or suborned by the enemy, but more often this happens when an operative 'goes native.' There are many routes to going native, but the most commonly encountered is when an operative develops close relationships with their assets or the country in which they are operating. For example, a case officer who is handling several local informants might develop a close relationship with one of them, which can cause complications.

An operative who has 'gone native' can still be useful to the network and their home country, but their loyalties will at the least be divided. It can be difficult to tell the difference between someone who is blending in well and someone who has gone native until they make some telling action – by which time it can be too late. The decision as to what to do with an operative who has gone native can be a tricky one. They may still be useful, in a reduced capacity, but once they realise they are being cut out of the loop they may become resentful. A disaffected former network member is a dangerous thing to leave in the field. Another hazard to networks is the danger of fratricide; the situation where two operations collide and interfere with one another. This can happen within a network, and is far more likely when different intelligence agencies are operating in the same area. Preventing fratricide is sometimes referred to as 'keeping the lines straight' but can be difficult when information is compartmentalised.

Access to information within a network should be on a 'need to know' basis. That is, personnel should only have access to information they need in order to fulfil their function. However, too little can be as dangerous as too much, though often in different ways. Sometimes 'good to know' (useful but not vital) information can be provided to assist personnel in keeping their lines straight or setting up an operation.

Operatives might also go about obtaining their own 'good to know' and 'nice to know' information if they think it is necessary or helpful. This can create a situation where several members of the network are running their own assets to try to fill in the blanks surrounding the data they have been given through official channels. Such a situation can lead to fratricide or a network being indirectly penetrated by hostile intelligence agencies.

One way to handle certain kinds of information is to 'black box' it. Black boxed information is to be trusted and treated as unquestionably accurate, but its source is never hinted at nor revealed. This can make some operatives nervous, especially if black boxed information has in the past turned out to be unreliable. Most information passed from one part of a network to another is black boxed for security reasons.

 There will be times where investigating Our Other Enemy reveals information useful for less esoteric matters. In these cases you should always 'black box' the information in order to keep the source secret. Do not do this if you fear that the source might be discovered in some way. Defeating Our Other enemy is of greater concern than serving some more mundane agenda. – Steuben

SOURCES AND ASSETS

The term 'source' is applied to anyone providing information to an operative. The term is extremely vague and can cover anything from a gossipy newspaper vendor to a high-value informant in the enemy's intelligence community. The term 'agent' is used for someone who acts on behalf of the intelligence services, such as a person who collects information or engages in spreading propaganda among dissidents, but is not one of our operatives. The term 'asset' is more generally used to mean anyone who is of value to the network.

 Be flexible in your network and assets. There is a greater issue at hand: in fact, two greater issues. No

potential asset is placed too far below your station to be used. This is one place where a disguise or alternative cover identity can be useful. There is no reason why a businessman on holiday needs to interact with a lowly street tough, but an opium runner certainly would. This also provides layers of security for your true mission and main cover. –N

The commonest use for assets is information gathering. Information of all sorts can be valuable, but two factors make one source more valuable than another: reliability and access. Reliability can be hard to judge; some sources may be working for enemy intelligence agencies, dangling some information as a lure to draw in our operatives. Others have their own agenda or are prone to invention. Reliability can be judged most accurately over time, but this luxury is not always available.

Access to useful information is what makes some assets more valuable than others. This is usually due to what is termed 'positioning'. Positioning is not so much about locality as it is contact with information flow and other sources. For example, two sources in the same city may not be of the same value if one has access to high-end information and the other can only report on mundane happenings.

Assets must always be considered expendable, and the network must be able to dissociate itself from one without being compromised. Each and every time an asset is used there is a risk they will be blown, so the decision to make use of a high-value asset is a difficult one. Some assets become 'sleepers' who may not be activated for many years, if ever.

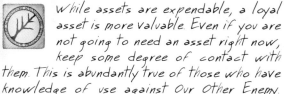

 While assets are expendable, a loyal asset is more valuable. Even if you are not going to need an asset right now, keep some degree of contact with them. This is abundantly true of those who have knowledge of use against Our Other Enemy. Such people are rare, which makes them doubly valuable. However, do not hesitate to cut one out if needed, even permanently. -N

Some sources are as valuable as they will ever be from the moment of first contact. This is particularly true of low-value informants or assets who are positioned in a way that is only useful under very specific circumstances. Others can be or must be developed once contact is made. This can mean building trust or developing a relationship with the asset, or convincing them by some means to work for the network. In some cases an asset can be developed by helping them insinuate themselves more closely into the target organisation.

In any region and field of interest, there is a 'centre of gravity'. This is the point where an asset can collect the most information – or the greatest quantity of valuable information – on a given subject for the least effort or outlay. An asset located close to the centre of gravity is extremely valuable. This does not necessarily translate to the most difficult to obtain: circumstances vary and the centre of gravity may not be in a place that is especially well secured.

RELIABILITY AND LEVERAGE

Sources and other assets vary considerably. The least reliable are those who simply want money for information – they will take money from other clients too. The 'true believer' can be a troublesome asset too. This is someone who believes passionately in a particular cause, which may be nothing whatsoever to do with why they are recruited as an intelligence asset. True believers can sometimes be induced to supply information to others who share their beliefs or support their agenda, but can be easily alienated if they are treated as cranks or their beliefs are belittled.

 Servants of Our Other Enemy can often be categorized as 'true believers', which can make them rather easy to manipulate if you can convince them that you are a fellow traveller. Easy, yes, but not safe by any means. Running a network of cattle is walking a razor's edge; any misstep and you become the target for their insanity. – Rodriguez

The most reliable sources are those who sympathise with us and want to help voluntarily, though it can be hard to tell if this is a real belief or a gambit on the part of a hostile agency. Some voluntary assets are not very useful even if they are reliable. For example, some countries are popular retirement destinations, or people from our home countries may have gone to live there and be willing to help our intelligence services. However, it is not all that likely that a retired merchant sailor (for example) will have access to much information of critical importance to us.

Coerced sources are usually the best in terms of reliability and, if selected well, usefulness. Coercion can take many forms. One common trick used by various intelligence services is to obtain photographs of the asset doing something that would harm his reputation, livelihood or safety. Sometimes an attractive person, termed a 'swallow' by some intelligence agencies, will seduce the target for the purpose of obtaining such photos. Of course, much depends on whether the target cares if his indiscretion is revealed.

It can be hard to turn someone whose lusts are for the bizarre symmetries of reality or who has seen horrors too tough to imagine. You can't bribe them, you can't seduce them, and you can't beat them into working for you. You can convince them you are one of them, though that has its risks. – Miller

Discrepancies in financial and business dealings, or crimes hidden in the target's past, are all potential leverage. So is a history of providing information to intelligence services. This means that once coerced into working for our network an asset continues to provide us with leverage for future use. However, it is possible to push an asset too far; if too much is asked they may refuse, or sell the network out. When this happens it is usually in return for escaping the consequences of their earlier actions.

SQUEEZING AND BURNING SOURCES

It may sometimes be necessary to 'squeeze' a source in order to get more from them than they want to give. This is easier where a source is coerced; one who is working for money may find it relatively easy to refuse an additional payment if they think the risk is too high or the task is too much trouble.

Thus, even if a source is simply working for payment it can be worthwhile finding some leverage to use if they need to be squeezed. The fact that they have provided information to a foreign intelligence operative for money might be sufficient, but it does require revealing to the source that they have done so.

SPOT RULES FOR RECRUITING ASSETS

Most often, the process of recruiting an asset is a major event, possibly providing the focus for a scenario or a chapter of a campaign. In such cases, the Keeper will want to play the process out over a number of scenes, with the investigators using a variety of skills as they gather information, plant incriminating evidence, set up honey traps or apply pressure to the right points of their recruit's life.

Occasionally, however, the Keeper may want to handle the recruitment simply in order to focus on a different strand of the campaign. In these cases, recruitment may simply be abstracted to a single roll that combines a number of skills. Some examples are:

- Planting false evidence and blackmailing the target: combined Stealth, Tradecraft and Intimidation.
- Determining whether the target is corrupt and offering a suitable bribe: Psychology, Tradecraft and one of Charm, Fast Talk or Persuade.
- Seducing and sexually blackmailing the target: Charm, Intimidate and Tradecraft.
- Discovering who or what the target cares about and threatening it: Psychology, Intimidate and Tradecraft.
- Appealing to the target's ego or ideology: Psychology, Tradecraft and one of Charm, Fast Talk or Persuade.

It may be preferable to find some other means to coerce them, which does not expose our operatives for what they are. All assets should be distanced from the network as much as possible. Information and instructions can be passed by dead drop (with no direct contact between the asset and his handler – see pg. 24), or by contact with a single member of the network. This way no asset can reveal much, whether voluntarily or otherwise. Ideally an asset should not know anything beyond the fact that he has done certain things for… someone. He should not know whether that someone is part of a huge network or is a solo operative, nor anything about the larger plans he is part of.

 Remember that your identity as an agent of a national intelligence service is the only thing allowing you to fight the good fight. Blowing that can be as easy as burning a network and not having a good explanation why. I'm not saying don't burn that network, I am just telling you to be prepared to justify it to your superiors. – Rodriguez

BUILDING A NETWORK

An intelligence network typically comprises several, loosely connected components. Wherever possible 'cut-outs' should be used; people who carry information and instructions

between the different parts of the network. If part of the network is compromised, the cut-out can disappear, ensuring that captured or suborned personnel have no idea how to contact the rest of the network. Of course, the enemy may be able to make an educated guess as to who is part of the network, perhaps by considering who has an identity that would make a good cover. If part of a network is compromised but the cut-out has worked, members may still be questioned. The enemy might claim to have proof of complicity, but this is unlikely to be true.

Most networks will not include analysis staff, since analysts need to know a great deal of information about many things in order to do their work. It is therefore far too risky to station them anywhere that they could be grabbed by the enemy. Similarly, cryptanalysts (who attempt to break enemy codes) are not stationed anywhere but friendly territory. Some low-level analysis and cryptography can be carried out on-site by staff who are part of a network, but those who specialise in such tasks are forbidden from entering enemy or even neutral territory.

CORE STAFF

The senior intelligence officer in a region is usually termed the Head of Station, and will often be a member of an embassy staff. If this is the case, they are – like all diplomatic personnel – what is termed 'legal'. This means that the opposition can expel them and refuse permission to return to their territory, but cannot imprison, interrogate or eliminate them without causing a diplomatic incident. 'Illegals', by this definition, are those who are not openly working for their home nation (in some capacity); they therefore have no protection if captured.

If the Head of Station and support staff are 'legal', then making contact with them can be problematic, although it does offer protection against key personnel being arrested and interrogated, and allows items to be moved in and out of the target country in a 'diplomatic bag'. Most 'illegal' networks will rarely, if ever, have contact with a legal Head of Station, instead relying on their own channels for communication.

 Our Other Enemy does not care about diplomatic immunity, 'legal' personnel at an embassy or mission, diplomatic bags or any of the safe means you are used to. -N

 Sometimes they are Our Other Enemy. - Miller

A network that does not fall under the control of the Head of Station will have its own commander and key personnel, who will not normally undertake work in the field. There will be one or more case officers who handle assets, plus experts who deal with communications or other critical tasks. Some networks might also have vehicle or intrusion specialists, linguists or other necessary personnel, though this is something of a luxury and is by no means common.

A network may have various field operatives attached to it. Some of these might have access to the network's headquarters, if it has one, whilst others might be kept at a distance for security reasons. These general personnel carry out a variety of tasks in the field, ranging from simple driving and security work, to surveillance and 'black bag' (breaking and entering) jobs. Some have no other function than to act as couriers to liaise with other parts of the network; they can serve as cut-outs as needed.

The Structure of a Network

A network that is larger than a couple of case officers and a commander will usually be subdivided in a manner not dissimilar to the way many insurgent forces are divided into self-contained 'cells'. Members of a cell will usually know (or at least have a reasonable idea) who one another are, but communication between cells is minimal and always by way of a cut-out. Ideally, members of a cell will not know how many other cells there are, let alone any details about them.

Cells can be organised in a variety of ways. The simplest is to have each reporting to a central 'command cell' by way of a cut-out. However, sometimes a cell will have command of one or more other cells, which report to it and have no direct contact with the command cell.

Cells can be organised by locality or by function, or as a combination of both. That is, a network might have a central command cell that controls two regional cells, one of which has a subordinate cell tasked with a specialist function such as watching a particular location. In addition, the command cell controls two local general/information-gathering cells and a specialist cell formed of field operatives who are moved around and given various tasks depending on what the other cells have learned. The loss of any of these cells, other than the command cell, would not cripple the network.

Recruiting Assets

A network must be built slowly and carefully. Some functions can be fulfilled by operatives sent from home, but it is not usually possible to send a whole network's worth of operatives and hope to avoid detection. Even the most obtuse of foreign intelligence agencies will notice something amiss if this is attempted. A network must instead be grown over time, with assigned personnel then beginning the task of developing local assets.

 When establishing your own network of assets, keep in mind that you are playing a double game. If an asset can be used both for agency and Other work, then do so. This is particularly easy with couriers, cut-outs and others who have no idea who they are working for or why. -N

The selection of potential assets is a tricky business. Intelligence agencies sometimes position their own personnel where they are likely to be approached, and even if this is not the case some potential assets may be spooked by an approach and alert the authorities. The selection and approach process is best compared to an assassination attempt: the assassin does not strike unless they are confident they can succeed. The same applies to approaching a potential asset.

There are exceptions to this rule. If our intelligence agencies are known to be interested in an area, then a deliberately ham-fisted approach to potential assets can actually be quite useful. The opposition can hardly fail to notice the efforts being made, which may serve to distract them from subtler operations elsewhere. They will also attempt to place personnel where these clumsy recruitment efforts will find them, which enables us to feed information to the opposition through operatives about whom they think we are ignorant.

However, for the most part potential assets must be carefully observed and evaluated long before an approach is made. Some of the factors that make an asset desirable can also make them a bad choice. Someone who is rabidly opposed to their government might be very willing to help us, but they will also attract attention – and will probably already have done so. Such people are best used as decoys or else left alone to cause a nuisance to the opposition by their own efforts.

It might be nearly impossible to turn one of the cattle into an asset. Few have interests outside their insanity that you can turn to your advantage. You can play on their devotion, especially the lower ranked and more ambitious members of a cell, by offering books, scrolls, or (fake) items of esoteric interest. A better target would be a person who, while not an intimate, has access to the cell's lair or other meeting place. The ritual chamber still needs electricity, and the house above likely has a telephone line. Food might be delivered, the leader of the cattle might have an accountant who handles their money, or the swimming pool might need to be cleaned. The most dangerous of servants of Our Other Enemy can maintain a façade of the mundane, and such a façade can be our way in. -N

Newcomers to the area of operations are best treated with suspicion. A new junior scientist who pops up at a location of interest just as we begin recruiting assets in the area might be a lucky find, but they are far more likely to be a plant for the enemy's intelligence services.

Newcomers are unlikely to be well positioned to obtain good information unless they are highly placed, in which case they may be very loyal or be under observation – or both. Obviously gaining someone in a high position as an asset is a coup, but it is a high-risk operation.

Walk-ins are also to be treated with suspicion. A walk-in is anyone who offers their services (usually but not always as an informant) without being approached. It should go without saying that a properly covert network will not be directly approached because nobody knows it is there, but sometimes local citizens will contact an embassy directly.

Alternatively, they may approach business representatives who have nothing to do with intelligence work, but might be able to put them in contact with someone who wants their services. If the network is in a friendly or neutral country then walk-ins often hope to be assisted in defecting in return for their services or information.

Walk-ins are to be treated not merely with suspicion, but with a higher degree of scrutiny than with operations against mundane targets. They represent a grave danger to Section 46. Even knowing about us is a sure sign of a security breach. Always assume that a walk-in is a servant of Our Other Enemy, and treat them accordingly. The most important piece of information you can acquire about a walk-in is how they even know about us. -N

Where genuine, walk-ins can be a godsend, but the prospect of being given something for nothing should alarm any intelligence operative. The potential asset's motivations might make them unreliable, or they might be under observation by the opposition – they could of course be an intelligence operative. It is possible to become so mesmerised by the possibilities created by this windfall that the operative fails to wonder if it is all too good to be true.

ASSESSING WALK-INS

While the Psychology skill may help assess the trustworthiness of a walk-in, it cannot be relied upon. If the walk-in is a skilled liar, the difficulty of the roll will at least be Hard, or possibly Extreme for a genuine master of deception. Even a success may not reveal for sure that the target is lying, given that the circumstances will probably make them nervous enough to make their reactions hard to assess.

The Keeper is encouraged to avoid simple rolls in circumstances such as these. Assessing the validity of a walk-in should be a process, requiring the investigators to poke around in the target's life, mounting surveillance, discreetly questioning acquaintances and searching through their belongings. If the walk-in is a plant from another agency, they will have gone to a great deal of effort to fabricate convincing evidence; testing its veracity could require some Hard rolls.

Once an individual has come to the attention of the network as a potential asset they must be evaluated. This is usually done by a combination of surveillance and digging into their background. Much can be learned about an individual from their habits. Small details like which paper they read or what brand of cigarettes they favour can be used to build a picture of their personality, and by observing these things an operative can determine what a foreign intelligence operative would see if he target attracted interest. A potential asset who might set alarm bells ringing with their daily habits should not be approached.

Financial matters are also of great interest. These can be investigated in many ways. One option is to obtain information directly either by observation or by gaining access to ledgers, receipts and so forth. Another is to use secondary sources, for example by investigating the shops and businesses the target buys from. A potential asset who is careless with their own money and prone to extravagant spending will more than likely do the same with funds earned working for our network. This could draw unwelcome attention. Heavy spending, especially beyond the target's means, might also indicate that they are corrupt or in financial trouble. This could make them vulnerable to coercion or bribery – or both – but also implies that they might be a security risk.

What an individual spends their money on can be telling in other ways. It may reveal that they are supporting someone – perhaps a sick relative or a child that nobody knows about, perhaps one or more mistresses – or is already paying blackmail to someone. It can also suggest weaknesses or areas of interest such as wine or art that can be made use of by an operative.

Before a potential asset is approached, their case officer should already be in possession of a complete profile. This must address all aspects of their life and personality, ranging from their taste in food and clothing to any interest in sport or culture. Not all of these details will seem relevant, but the facts do add up and something that was overlooked as trivial might turn out to be very important indeed. Most importantly, the profile will indicate whether the individual is worth the risk of an approach

No matter how much effort has been put into assessing an individual, it is always necessary to be willing to abandon the effort if the risks are too great or the benefits too small. For example, investigation into a potentially useful asset might reveal that although they have a 'big title', they are actually of little importance and have access to no information of any real worth. Tempting as it might be to proceed with an approach just in case the asset turns out to be more useful than expected, if the risk is not justified by a realistic prospect of worthwhile gains then the operation must be terminated.

PRE-APPROACH

It is sometimes possible to make a pre-approach in order to sound out the potential asset. This should be carried out by someone the asset will not encounter again whilst involved with the network, and they must not realise that anything has happened. The pre-approach could take the form of a chance encounter with an attractive person in a bar, a few moments of shared grumbling with a kindred spirit whilst waiting for a train, or some similar innocuous situation.

APPROACH

If the pre-approach goes well and the potential asset responds in a suitable manner to a few loaded phrases, then the actual approach can go ahead. This is the most dangerous moment of all, and is often preceded by a period in which the subject is befriended or a working relationship is developed under the pretence of more normal business or social interaction.

The Pitch

At some point, however, it is necessary to take the plunge and make 'the pitch'. How this is done depends very much on the assessment of the individual. In some cases, especially where the subject is to be bribed or coerced, a straightforward and businesslike approach may be best. This may be accompanied by a certain amount of hostility if the subject is being coerced and it is deemed necessary to make them fear the consequences of non-compliance. However, even in the case where coercion using the threat of violence is the chosen method, operatives may find it more effective to be civil and matter-of-fact about the situation.

Where a subject is to be suborned or seduced (not necessarily in a sexual context) into working for the network, a friendly or at least civil approach is definitely necessary. It may be possible to present the situation as a business arrangement, with a clear agreement on what is to be given in return for what – though of course our end of the deal need not be honest! However, some subjects may find this approach distasteful. Someone who is helping us because they despise their own government or out of some similar idealism will not like their grand gesture being treated as a business transaction.

This does not necessarily mean that some form of roundabout bargaining will not take place; it almost certainly will. However, it will be couched in idealistic and high-minded terms that allow the subject to pretend that he is not negotiating a price for his treachery.

With or without this sort of self-delusion, it is wise to mislead the subject about who they are going to be working for or what they will be expected to do. If the asset later finds out that they have been lied to they may become disaffected, but this risk is usually outweighed by the fact that they do not know who they have been reporting to. Similarly, it is generally easier to persuade someone to betray their country or employer in a small way than on a grand scale. Once the subject has become inured to the idea, or they have incriminated themselves and can be coerced, then they can be squeezed as necessary to force them into greater acts of subversion.

Procurement and Facilitation

Exactly what will bring a given individual under the network's control can vary considerably. Some will sign up voluntarily because they think they are helping a friend or furthering their ideals. Some want to win the approval of someone they admire or are attracted to. Some can be controlled through fear and others through bribery with money or sex. Some

have a particular weakness or need that, if located, will give us control over them where normally they would be incorruptible. It is worth restating that the correct approach must be planned beforehand and this requires a lengthy period of preparation. A failed attempt at subversion can result in an operative or even a whole network being blown, so caution is absolutely necessary.

Appeals to self-interest and greed can vary considerably, and as a rule the more sophisticated the bribe has to be, the more reliable the subject. Someone who is willing to betray a trust for cash is probably not all that trustworthy, whereas a subject who needs money to pay off a debt or to help someone else (such as obtaining medical assistance for a relative) will typically be a person of 'better' character and less likely to try to change the deal or to seek additional bribes elsewhere.

Offers of money may have to be couched in other terms, especially when dealing with an idealist or a corrupt and self-serving individual who somehow considers themselves to be better than everyone else. In such cases procurement or facilitation might offer a more palatable alternative to bribery, though it amounts to the same thing. Someone who would not take money might be willing to accept the promise of a necessary medical procedure for a relative, or to be handed fake passports to get their children out of the country.

Procurement and facilitation are very similar. Procurement refers to obtaining something the subject wants or will be so delighted by that they will be amenable to requests, whilst facilitation refers to making something possible for him. A man with a love of cars might be won over by the procurement of a particular model; one whose interests are more carnal can be bribed by facilitating his sexual proclivities.

It is possible to build on this procurement/facilitation relationship until the subject becomes dependent on our operatives to obtain the things they want and have come to expect. It then becomes possible to coerce the subject by threatening to end the relationship. In addition to influencing the subject to act for us, this also gives them a strong incentive not to betray the network or even to actively protect it.

Note also that operatives cannot afford to be concerned with the effects of subversion on the subject. Someone who betrays their country or some other trust risks a dire fate, but that is not our concern. Operatives must be willing to coerce or suborn individuals in the full knowledge that they are thereby placed in great danger in the long or short term. Let us not forget that these people are helping us for their own reasons and are not necessarily our friends. They are also corrupt, or traitors, or guilty of something; but none of that matters.

HANDLING PROCUREMENT AND FACILITATION

If an investigator is attempting to use procurement or facilitation techniques to recruit a new asset, the first stage is to find out what the potential recruit desires. An investigator attempting to discover this through conversation may use a combined roll against Psychology and either Charm or Fast Talk, depending on the approach. If the investigator is attempting to piece this together from research, this instead calls for a combined Psychology and Tradecraft roll.

In most cases, an investigator is able to call upon the resources of their agency to furnish the means to tempt a potential asset. There are exceptions, however. If the potential recruit is making unreasonable demands, such as much larger amounts of money than the agency would normally pay, the investigator may make a Trust roll to secure these resources. Time pressures may also preclude going through official channels, in which case the investigator may be forced to find alternative sources.

While an officer should never be expected to use their own finances, and doing so may risk operational security, Credit Rating may still be appropriate for having useful contacts or the proper bearing to operate in certain social circles. An investigator may roll against Credit Rating to identify people who can supply items such as luxury cars or high-quality drugs, and then use the appropriate social skills or outright theft to obtain them. Catering to a potential recruit's sexual desires may involve a Tradecraft roll to have suitable contacts, Credit Rating to hire a high-class prostitute or Charm to talk a suitable individual into whatever is required.

The only factors that matter are that the subject is useful and available. That said, operatives still need to consider the consequences for anyone they recruit as an asset. Not for humanitarian or friendly reasons, but because it may affect what the subject is willing to do, and how useful they can be. Blatantly recruiting and using people is only viable in the short term, and can draw unwelcome attention. Thus the fate of the asset does matter, in that it can have an effect on future operations. This is the only reason it can matter, however. A case officer who cares too much about their assets has gone native and may become a liability.

Finally, it should be noted that the best way to make use of a given individual may not be to suborn or coerce them directly. An official's wife, mistress or friend might be a better choice as an asset than the official themselves. They may be able to obtain information from the subject even though they would never divulge it even under torture; the same goes for obtaining documents, keys and the like from the subject, who might never find out that they are the source of the leak they are investigating.

Making someone close to an important subject an asset has one other potential use; it can be used to gain leverage to coerce them. Someone who would never betray a trust to save themselves might be entirely willing to work for us in return for not turning in their loved ones. Handled properly, this approach can be used to 'trade up' assets by suborning someone of relatively low value and getting them to do something that would land them in trouble if discovered. Once the true subject compromises themselves to protect a loved one, they become vulnerable to a direct approach.

PERSONAL MEETINGS

Contact between members of the network is hazardous unless it is covered by the operatives' assumed identities. Obviously, if two operatives have cover identities that work in the same building or for the same firm, then being seen together is unlikely to arouse suspicion. Under most other circumstances a face-to-face meeting is an occasion of increased risk. Even a previously reliable asset could make a mistake or might have been 'turned' by the opposition. Often intelligence services will offer minor assets a deal whereby they are treated leniently in return for exposing their contacts.

Some personal meetings are unavoidable. It may be necessary to call key personnel together for a planning session or a briefing, though wherever possible orders are disseminated to those requiring them without everyone having to be in the same place. Not only is it hard to create a cover story for such a gathering or to conceal it from notice, but it is best if most network members never meet and therefore cannot identify one another.

A suitable cover story must exist for any personal meeting. This need not be complex; a businessman who visits an upmarket bar in the evening and chats with a couple of other patrons is hardly anything out of the ordinary. However, everyone must be able to explain their presence at the meeting spot. If any operative attracts attention then others they have met with may also be questioned.

 If your assets are fairly separate from each other in time and space, you can use the same cover for both, if it fits. Just remember that time and space are relative. Nothing is worse than running two assets under the same cover and having both of them walk into the bar while you are working with a third. – Miller

The choice of meeting spot depends greatly upon the activity that is to take place. A quick exchange of objects, such as a handgun or an envelope containing cash or instructions, can be carried out anywhere there is suitable concealment. If a lengthy conversation is necessary then the location must offer both a plausible reason for stopping there and some measure of privacy. Most meetings must take place in public areas, for various reasons. Somewhere that has people coming and going all the time is a reasonable choice, but crowds cause too many problems. A quiet bar, café or restaurant is a reasonable choice, or perhaps the waiting room of a small railway station. Obviously, the more times a meeting spot is used the greater the risk, so meeting places – and times – must be varied as much as possible.

Operatives must be mindful that the authorities are not the only threat. Random passers-by might report people behaving suspiciously or might even take exception to what they think is going on. Operatives do not want any sort of attention, and while cover stories such as meeting a prostitute or something similar are useful in some areas, local conditions may make this a poor choice.

Care must be taken to act naturally throughout the meeting. Observers will be a lot less suspicious of people who smile or laugh as if enjoying a social conversation than of people who speak quietly and furtively; as always it is important to act appropriately for the surroundings. Other factors that might stand out to an observer include an operative who looks impatient before a 'chance meeting' takes place. Little

things that seem slightly 'off' can provide the opposition with enough clues to compromise a network. Operatives should always be alert for surveillance or other risks when approaching a meeting, and should be willing to abort the contact and leave the area of he is suspicious. When a meeting between a high-value operative and someone from outside the network is required, it is advisable to use a cut-out to bring the contact from an initial meeting to a secondary site, or to intercept the contact en route to the meeting. This may avoid any hostile surveillance or snatch squad waiting at the contact location.

Operatives should not, under any circumstances, meet a contact at a place and time of the contact's choosing unless they are absolutely sure of their trustworthiness. All meetings should be on the operative's own terms and the time and place should not be provided prematurely. It is acceptable to tell the contact when but not where at the time the meeting is set up, with the location provided at the last minute. Alternatively, the contact might be told when and where to pick up the details of the meeting, ensuring that he cannot feed them to the enemy in advance.

INFORMERS AND DOUBLE AGENTS

There are many reasons why a network member might start working for the enemy or an asset might inform on a handler. Greed, disaffection over how he has been treated or with the Western world in general, pressure from foreign intelligence agencies, even just a falling-out with someone can be a cause. Assets have been known to betray their handlers for the most petty of reasons, and ultimately the reasons are less important than the betrayal.

One way to deter betrayal is the use – or threat – of a network's enforcers. These may or may not actually exist, but if the asset thinks that the network has personnel whose sole task is to hurt or kill them if they misbehave, they are more likely to stay on the straight and narrow. Killing a suspected informant does solve the immediate problem but the body must be disposed of and of course the opposing intelligence community may draw conclusions from his disappearance. It is sometimes more useful to arrange for the informant to be dealt with by local criminals or to set them up to look like they have betrayed another group and allow them to deal with the problem.

 DISPOSING OF BODIES

See pg. 85 for details of disposing of bodies safely and thoroughly.

This is a rather extreme case, and knowing why an asset might turn informer can help prevent it from happening or enable a network to dissociate itself in time to avoid damage. Most assets lack finesse so it can be fairly obvious when the behaviour of one changes. More dangerous is the double agent, who pretends to be working for one side but is actually feeding information to the enemy.

Although dangerous to the network these informers can be useful. A known informer can be fed incorrect or misleading information. If this is obviously damaging to the enemy the informer may be eliminated by them, solving a security problem for the network. However, it may be possible to play an informant more subtly, by giving them access to information that is mostly correct but not very useful to the enemy. Once the informant is trusted, they can be used to feed disinformation directly to the enemy; even if they are perceived as unreliable this can be useful.

If the enemy believes an informant is reliable, they will act upon what the informant says. If, on the other hand, the informant is sometimes wrong, the enemy will seek corroboration or fail to act at all. The unreliability of one informant can undermine confidence in others. Even if an informant is not useful as a conduit for false information, they can still be used to confuse the enemy and cloud the issue.

At times it may be necessary to remind an asset or even an operative that there are consequences for inappropriate conduct. Some assets will brag about their involvement in covert activities or start making stupid errors through complacency, and may need correction. Often this need be nothing more than 'polite threats' but it may eventually become necessary to discipline or even eliminate part of the network to prevent a security breach. If an asset or operative is about to be captured and cannot be removed from the situation, the only option may be to kill them before they can talk.

One other benefit of a known informant is that the enemy will be unlikely to expend much effort on placing another informant within our network if they already have one. So long as the informant is carefully watched and fed only non-damaging information, the opposition may well be satisfied with the situation. If the enemy does not realise we know about their informant they may underestimate our capabilities.

It may be possible to 'turn ' an informant or leak within the network, creating a double, triple or quadruple agent – though there does come a point where it is impossible to say for sure whose side a given individual is on. This often happens when someone gets into the habit of making whatever deal he thinks will save him from the latest threat, creating layers of promises to help both sides and reveal any attempts to coerce or turn him by other agencies.

A turned informant is slightly different to one who is detected but eliminated. The latter is deliberately lied to whereas the former is, theoretically, cooperating voluntarily. Some of the information they give to the opposition must be accurate enough to satisfy them. If the flow of information stops or the data passed on is always worthless, the enemy will realise

Never hesitate to sacrifice a network in order to achieve victory over Our Other Enemy. All too often the schemes of servants of Our Other Enemy can lead to world-shattering consequences. Such a threat pales in comparison to the mundane concerns of national interests. Burn an asset or even a whole network of them. Make sacrifices, even the supreme one. -N

Though it is far better to sacrifice another than yourself. Live to fight another day and you do more harm to Our Other Enemy than simply dying for the cause. Let the fanatics die for theirs. – Steuben

that their informant has been detected. To remain useful the informant must still provide at least some truthful intelligence.

ASSESSING UNRELIABLE AGENTS

By the time a triple-agent reaches the stage where they are saying whatever they believe their handlers want to hear, it can be difficult to get any kind of read on them. The agent is so used to lying that it has become easier than telling the truth or, worse, they may start to believe their own lies. Psychology rolls against such targets should always be set at least one degree of difficulty higher than the target's opposing skill level would normally dictate. In the case of opposed rolls, the investigator gains a penalty die.

The informant must be considered expendable, and even if they are led to believe that they have been returned to a position of trust within the network they can never again be trusted with important information.

PLANNING OPERATIONS AND OPERATIONAL ORDERS

Before planning any sort of operation, and repeatedly during the planning process, the question of risk versus reward must be addressed. At times, doing nothing is the best option for a network if the enemy has an ongoing security alert. In fact, a network without any ongoing operations is still not 'doing nothing'; it is remaining covert and ensuring that it continues to be available when needed. A network that is compromised over a trivial operation has been lost for no real gain.

When planning an operation, the value of the eventual goal must be weighed against the consequences of a failed operation – and also a successful one. A minor operation that succeeds but results in an increased level of vigilance might not have been worth it. Operatives might be willing to risk their own lives but there are wider considerations.

Defeating Our Other Enemy is the only thing of concern; all the rest is window dressing to enable that great work to be carried out. –N

A blown op can result in the loss of several operatives; arguably this may be acceptable, but the network is a strategic asset that will take a long time to replace. Each time it is hazarded there is a risk that this asset will be gone forever. Few operations are worth the certain loss of part or all of a network. Planners must balance the potential rewards against the risk to the network. Such risks can be reduced by the use of cells and cut-outs, or by using expendable assets to carry out the dangerous parts of the mission. Planning an operation takes place in several stages. A partial plan may be formed, highlighting what information and equipment is required for the operation. An assessment of how these might be obtained can lead to the plan being scrapped and a new one formulated.

Target Selection may be dictated by orders from elsewhere, or the network's command staff may spot a potential target whilst working through information gathered routinely by the network. For example, routine observation of a naval dockyard might indicate that schematics for the Soviet Navy's attack submarines are held there. Obtaining these would be valuable to Western navies and strategic planners, so this might be a mission worth undertaking.

Preliminary Reconnaissance and Assessment may already be partially complete at this phase; routine observation may have already yielded much of the necessary data. This must still be confirmed, especially if the observations are not recent, and any gaps in the necessary data must be filled. All manner of information may be useful at this stage, but security procedures and means of access to the target are of paramount importance. At this stage the feasibility of the operation is assessed, leading to a 'scrap, shelve or set up' decision. If the operation seems to offer a reasonable balance of risk to gain, the network's commanders can proceed to the set-up stage.

Setting Up an operation can be a complex business, and may require resources or personnel that are unavailable to the network. Additional personnel or equipment can be requested, but this takes time and requires the situation be re-evaluated once they are available. Local assets or locally available resources such as cars, uniforms and the like must also be obtained. Gaining assets in place is a lengthy business, whereas activating an asset already in place is much quicker. Generic items such as tools and weapons can be obtained well ahead of time, but where grabbing an item or person would alert the opposition this can only be done immediately before or during the actual operation. At the set-up phase, operatives must obtain all necessary information to make these 'facilitating actions' as quick and simple as possible, but must do so in such a way as to not alert the opposition.

Once all the pieces are in place, reconnaissance continues as the network waits for the right opportunity. If necessary, a stand-down order can be given right up to the initiation of the final operation. As a rule, ops gain 'psychological momentum' as they advance through the planning and set-up phases, making a decision to abort much more difficult to make. However, it is the duty of the network's commanders to shelve an operation if necessary. No matter how much time and effort has been invested, standing down always remains an option. It may be the best choice in the long term.

REQUESTING RESOURCES

 Trust rolls may be required when requesting resources for an operation, but only if these resources are notably unusual or expensive (budgets are especially tight in British intelligence at this time), or if getting them to the investigators involves risk to other officers or agents. Reasonable requests for money, information or equipment should be granted as a matter of course.

Final Reconnaissance is the last set of reports before the launch order is given. Sometimes this is a deliberate measure, such as when the network's commander requests a final recon or report to ensure that nothing significant has changed. On other occasions the final recon may be a routine report that indicates conditions are right for the operation – or that something has arisen that requires an immediate launch or abort. Final recon can sometimes overlap (deliberately or otherwise) with the facilitation sub-operations.

HANDLING RECONNAISSANCE

 In most cases, the Keeper will probably want to play out reconnaissance as a scene, calling for skill rolls as appropriate. If the operation is not an integral part of the scenario, an alternative is to simply abstract it to a combined Tradecraft and Spot Hidden roll (or Tradecraft and Signals, Listen or other appropriate skill, depending on the form the reconnaissance takes).

Facilitation is the final stage before an operation begins, and some facilitating elements can only be carried out whilst the main mission is underway. Facilitation includes such measures as kidnapping a keyholder, obtaining a vehicle or uniforms that are likely to be missed before too long, and other necessary tasks that cannot be carried out in the set-up phase. This includes moving an exfiltration team into position or 'putting the squeeze' on an asset to obtain assistance. Facilitation is the last point where all operatives can be ordered to stand down, and as a rule the enemy will realise that something has happened if this is the case. Aborting at this stage is frustrating for everyone involved and can pose its own dangers.

HANDLING FACILITATION

 It is probably more interesting to play these actions out fully, but they may also be abstracted. A kidnapping may require a combined Stealth and Fighting (Brawl) roll, and stealing resources such as uniforms could be handled by a combined Stealth and Locksmith roll (Electronics could potentially take the place of Locksmith for more modern security systems). Tradecraft should only be combined with such rolls if the targets are trained in Tradecraft themselves.

The **Primary Mission** is whatever the planners intend it to be. It may be possible to add secondary objectives to a mission, but an excess of goals can make an operation unwieldy or just plain unworkable. The primary mission should always be worth all the effort put into it, even if no secondary goals are achieved, and must be accomplished no matter what success or failure is encountered on secondary goals. Planners must avoid the temptation to expand a mission during the various stages of its planning and execution. The goal must be set from the outset. Changing a the primary mission goal requires going back to the beginning of the planning phase and creating a new mission with a new objective.

EXFILTRATION, EXPLOITATION AND CLEAN-UP

No mission should be considered without a definite plan for how the operatives are to be extracted from the mission area and protected afterwards. If personnel are to leave the country or the region, this must be planned for in advance. Ways of avoiding any security measures triggered by the operation must also be thought out. This includes personnel who are not involved with the operation and may know nothing about it, but whose activities might be detected by a security force on alert. Planners must consider the implications of the operation for all personnel, not just those involved. Similarly, there must be a plan to exploit success. If documents are obtained, they must be conveyed to intelligence analysts. Snatched personnel must be held somewhere, interrogated and passed on or dealt with. Word of success must sometimes be passed back to intelligence chiefs back home. Similarly, the network must 'clean up' after the operation. This includes disposing of cars, weapon, tools and perhaps bodies in a manner that will not lead the opposition to network members if they are discovered.

Clean-up might be the most important part of any of our operations against Our Other Enemy. Disposing of bodies, destroying evidence of your presence and such should be routine for you. However, you will also need to sanitise the occult situation. Retrieve or destroy artefacts and books of interest. Obliterate any ritual items or symbols used by the cattle. Witnesses may also need to be eliminated and, sadly, victims of a cell often are too far damaged mentally and emotionally to be left in the care of medical personnel. Do what you have to do, even if it is one of your fellow operatives. Clean it all. -N

An operation is not complete, and should not be considered successful, until the gains are in the right hands and all personnel are as safe as possible from repercussions. This can take time, and an operational plan might include a lengthy period of reduced activity.

COMPARTMENTALISATION AND OPERATIONAL SECURITY

Operational security (OPSEC) is vital to the survival of any network, and one of the key tools is compartmentalisation. Compartmentalisation of tasks, compartmentalisation of information… compartmentalisation of everything that can be compartmentalised. The basic rule is "don't ask, don't tell."

Some planners need to know everything that is going on in order to put together a workable plan or to ensure that operations do not collide. Everyone else gets information on a 'need to know' basis. This is a standard procedure but operational security goes further than this. Personnel conducting parts of an operation may not know what the overall plan is, but the fact that they are active can be an indicator that something is about to happen. If the opposition spots this then a heightened alert state may ensue even if the target of the operation is not deduced. Timing is an essential part of operational security. If a part of the operation can be carried out without much chance of detection then the plan needs to allow time for a 'slow and quiet' execution. If it is likely to trigger an alert then this needs to be left as late as possible, leaving enough time to complete the sub-operation.

Actions that must be carried out whilst the main operation is already underway, such as procuring a vehicle for exfiltration and getting it into position, are risky. There is the possibility that the sub-op will fail whilst the main op is already committed, perhaps leaving the operatives with no means of escape or with a critical obstacle still in place. There is also the risk that if the timings do not mesh properly the sub-op may be detected and compromise the main operation.

Good planning and competent execution can remove a lot of these risks, though they are never completely eliminated. Over-compartmentalisation can cause its own problems. Personnel with little information cannot reveal it (deliberately or otherwise) but this does not mean they will not unknowingly take some action that compromises the mission. Planners must balance the need to keep secrets with the requirement to give personnel the information they need not only to carry out their mission but also to avoid accidental security breaches. Some personnel, at least, need to have enough information that they can make informed decisions in the field if the operation goes awry or central control breaks down. Compartmentalisation of tasks is desirable. For example, if the mission is to shoot a target, the mission personnel might be subdivided into a diversionary group, a gun carrier and an assassin. The 'gun carrier' conveys the weapon from storage and passes it to the assassin soon before they are due to strike, then disappears. If they are caught with the weapon then they cannot reveal the target. Likewise, the diversionary group might not know the target. Another group whose task is to get the assassin into the target's vicinity can do so and then withdraw, reducing the number of personnel exposed to risk when the trigger is pulled.

Operational Orders

Orders are yet another form of communication, and one that must be mastered by network commanders. Indeed, anyone who instructs someone else – an asset or another operative, or a cell within the network – to carry out any task must be familiar with how to present orders that are clear and easy to follow. The last thing a network needs is assets and operatives fumbling around trying to figure out what they are supposed to be doing.

Good orders are especially important when dealing with outsiders. Assets, local militia, insurgents and similar may not have an understanding of procedure and will make basic mistakes, especially if they misinterpret something that seems obvious to the planners. Military and law enforcement personnel are better at following instructions, but there is still room for error. This is especially true when working with organisations that have standard ways of thinking and acting. Certain words have very different meanings to members of various services, so terminology must always be used with due care and attention. Similarly, personnel used to civilian law enforcement procedures will act differently to those cleared for action in a war zone.

Orders must be given in a format that presents personnel with what they need to know, what we want them to do, and what we want them not to do. Additional information and details need to be clear and concise.

Orders may be delivered in written form or in a face-to-face briefing, as required. Standing orders can also be triggered by a signal or code phrase. The most risky – in terms of orders becoming garbled – form of transmission is when a third party has to pass the orders on. It is not always possible to acknowledge receipt of orders or to verify their authenticity, nor to obtain clarification if their orders do not seem to fit the circumstances. This is a risk inherent in intelligence work, which can be managed by good procedures, but never eliminated.

The planners will create a full set of operational orders, but this will not be made known to most (or perhaps any) of the personnel carrying out the mission. Once the complete plan is laid out and checked for likely problems, orders for all of the compartmentalised sections of the operation can be created and passed to those carrying out the component parts. It should be stressed that the parts must be derived form a coherent whole; trying to create an operation by writing orders for all the component parts and hoping they fit together at the end is a recipe for disaster.

A good set of operational orders will include the following:

- The purpose of the mission and intended outcome.
- Likely consequences of both success and failure.
- Personnel required to carry out the mission.
- Equipment, information and other items are needed to facilitate the mission.
- The location and circumstances under which the mission is to be carried out.
- Facilitation sub-operations necessary to make the mission feasible.
- The mission plan itself.
- Additional information as necessary including any circumstances to be avoided.
- Contingency orders, such as alternate exfiltration methods.

Once these operational orders are ready, personnel can be given their individual and small-group orders. There is usually no need to include very detailed information in these orders, but the main set of operational orders will indicate if and when information is necessary.

The following standard 5-heading format for orders should be used for individual orders:

- Information
- Intention
- Method
- Administration
- Inter-Communication

Information includes as much detail as is necessary on the target or objective of the mission (or the operative's part in it), but operatives should not be given information that they do not need. They may also be informed in a general sense about other things that will be going on, such as the fact that there will be a diversion while they enter the target building. Operatives should not know precise details unless they are needed for their mission role.

Intention is an indication of the intent of the operative's mission. Security must be balanced against the morale benefits of knowing an operative's place in a larger scheme. Generally it will suffice to outline the general aim of the mission and the importance of each operative's part in making the larger whole work.

Method is a detailed set of instructions for what each operative is to do, how and when. The method must include what means (weapons, explosives, apparently accidental damage) are to be used, how to get by enemy security, how to reach the target and how to get away afterwards. Timings are essential. Where possible, each operative should know only their own part in the mission and any details necessary to cooperate with his fellows.

Administration covers facilitation of the mission with such matters as weapons supply, transportation, documentation and other necessary items, and the identity of any contacts to be met with. Measures for dealing with casualties and dispersing after the mission will also be included in this section as well as the cover story if the operation is not overt.

Inter-Communication describes the means of communicating during the operation. There may be none; once an operative is committed to their part of the mission he will be expected to carry it out without further guidance. If communication is deemed necessary then this section will spell out how it is to be accomplished and any security arrangements surrounding it.

SAFE HOUSES AND OTHER LOCATIONS

The term 'safe house' can promote a dangerous way of thinking. There are no completely safe places, and each time a location is used there is a chance that it will be discovered by the opposition. However, the term 'safe house' is used for any location deemed secure enough to be used for meetings, storage of equipment or to house operatives and assets. A network's headquarters might also be considered a safe house, but would not normally be used to shelter operatives or assets, as this risks expose it. In a large network there may be several personnel whose sole task is to protect and operate safe houses. It is often necessary to create an atmosphere of normalcy about a location, so houses need to be lived in, businesses operated and so forth. Safe house personnel are usually armed or have weapons available. Some other locations are given the term 'safe house' with varying degrees of reliability. For example, a network that needs to hide someone quickly might persuade a local asset to provide a safe house – perhaps their own home. How safe this locality is can vary considerably.

Other locations can be used to store equipment and vehicles until needed, and may be the base for a specialist cell within the network. Such a cell might only have one or two members.

Examples include a mechanic and a facility for altering the appearance of vehicles, or an armoury that is the base for an explosives expert. Most networks do not have the luxury of such facilities. In an emergency they can be used as a safe house, but the facility must then be moved in case it is compromised.

We simply do not have the resources to provide you with your own safe houses, extractions and other support. You will receive what we can give you, but you have been chosen because of your ability to work outside of close support of management. This is why you are piggybacking on another mission, after all. -N

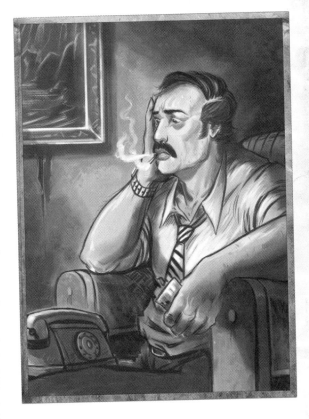

Some networks have a 'final' safe house whose sole purpose is to facilitate the escape of key network members if the authorities are closing in. Such facilities are something of a luxury and even if they exist will not be used for a single operative – once used, such a critical facility must be considered expended and a new one set up. Most operatives will not know of the existence of such an 'escape house', and the network leadership will generally prefer to allow a compromised operative to be caught rather than risk their emergency escape route. This is not merely for selfish reasons: the enemy must be denied access to the highest-value personnel even if the rest of the network is lost. Few networks are large enough to have many – if any – specialist facilities, but most should have at least one safe house prepared before any operation, and should try to maintain one for contingencies even when there is no operation in the offing. Circumstances vary considerably, however, and a network that has all the facilities its personnel would like to have is probably wasting resources that would be better put to use elsewhere. It is a sad fact of intelligence work that all operations run on a shoestring budget, and creativity is

necessary where resources are inadequate. Which is to say, always.

 If you are of the better sort, you might be tempted to use your own resources in this fight. Do not give into that temptation, for it can be all too easy to trace such expenditures back to you. As much as it pains me to say this, you must simply learn to live within the means of your cover, even if that entails less than ideal lodging or provisions. —Steuben

LOCATING A SAFE HOUSE

 Access to safe houses is normally arranged ahead of time. If an investigator needs to find a safe house in an emergency situation, much will depend on the lines of communication open to them.

If the investigator can contact their direct superior or handler in the intelligence services, and the request is a reasonable one, no roll is usually required. One exception may be if the investigator is operating in hostile or sparsely populated territory, with insufficient preparation, in which case the Keeper may call for a Luck roll for there to be a suitable safe house within easy reach.

If the investigator is relying on other colleagues within the intelligence services, such as the local Head of Station, and the safe house has not been pre-arranged, then a Trust roll may be required. The Keeper may ask for a Hard roll if the investigator makes this request of a member of an allied intelligence service instead of their own.

Approaching agents to provide a safe house is riskier. If the agent is a member of another organisation, the Keeper may ask for a Trust roll, adjusting the difficulty level depending on the investigator's approach

and whether they are being hunted by the authorities. If the agent is not allied with any group, an interpersonal skill roll will be more appropriate.

As a last-ditch effort, the investigator may attempt to bribe, coerce or convince an acquaintance or even a stranger to provide shelter and resources. Depending on the approach the investigator takes, this may call for a Charm, Fast Talk, Intimidate or Persuade roll. The difficulty should be Hard for someone the investigator knows, but who does not fully trust them, and Extreme for a stranger. Suitable threats, bribes, flirtation or similar may afford the investigator a bonus die. In these circumstances, failure does not necessarily mean that the target refuses the investigator's request for help; they may take the investigator in and then call the authorities, or look for a way to use the investigator for their own purposes.

In a populated environment, an investigator almost always has the option of taking shelter in a vacant building, but this will not offer the access to supplies, communications and medical help that a well-prepared safe house affords. An investigator should make a Luck roll to find a suitable building in an emergency.

Aeroplane travel is faster, but the train is much safer. Less official eyes on a train, and you can scarper easier if things go wrong, wrong. It also gives you time for a breather. Not that it is safe, nowhere is safe any more. On a long trip you should get a sleeper. You can hole up in a cabin. Gives you time to sleep and read, read. - Stanton

CHAPTER THREE

FIELD OPERATIONS

·FIELD OPERATIONS·

Almost any activity undertaken by operatives outside a safe house or network headquarters can be considered a 'field operation'. It must never be forgotten that something as simple as going out to buy a sandwich and a newspaper entails significant risk when undertaken in a hostile country, using a false identity. However, minor tasks and day-to-day activities can more properly be considered routine, requiring no more than maintenance of the cover identity. Such tasks can be carried out by someone with no training beyond an ability to assume a false identity. Many field operations, however, require more specialist skills or additional considerations.

OPERATING IN THE COUNTRYSIDE

Operations in the countryside can be more complex than many city-dwellers might imagine. Distances tend to be greater between places of interest, and the links between them are rarely good. Roads tend to be narrow and twisty, and if there is a rail service at all it will be intermittent. Thus simply getting from one place to another can pose challenges that would not exist in the urban environment.

Weather tends to have a greater influence on activities in the countryside. Extremes of weather can bring down trees, wash out roads or demolish bridges, but even fairly mild weather can cause problems. In a town or city, people will typically still go abroad during a heavy rainstorm because the pace of life rarely slows – it is still necessary to go to

work, theatre tickets cannot be returned and so forth – but someone tramping about in the open will stand out in the countryside. Of course, there are tasks that require country dwellers to go abroad in bad weather, but it is common to build a schedule around the weather rather than ignore it. Someone who acts differently will stand out.

This presupposes that the operative is in the relatively benign countryside of Western Europe. Getting cold and wet is unpleasant, and the weather can put very real obstacles in the way of an operation, but these are minor considerations compared to the very real dangers of operating in an area with limited water, venomous snakes, wild animals and other serious threats. It is quite possible to die of cold in the snow of the Polish winter or from thirst by a track in Angola without ever crossing an enemy agent.

 You don't have to go as far as Siberia to get away from the relatively safe countryside of Europe. There are plenty of places in Eastern Europe, especially in Romania and Hungary, that can pose a problem. By far the worst is being stuck in the middle of North America during a blizzard; no trees, roads buried and not a single landmark in sight. – Rodriguez

Rural communities are small, and most people will know one another by sight. Strangers will often stand out as a result of their speech, dress and mannerisms but even if

they do not they will not be recognised. In a town or city, it is nothing out of the ordinary to meet a person you do not know. In a small village, it may actually seem more suspicious if the operative does blend in; someone who is making an effort to seem like a local but who is known not to be might arouse suspicion where an obvious visitor with a plausible cover story would not.

Many rural populations are hostile to outsiders. Locals might be suspicious of 'townies' for reasons unrelated to espionage. All manner of social ills can lead to resentment even if the locals have nothing to hide, and some may also be engaged in illegal activity ranging from under-declaring property for tax or unlicensed distilling There is also the possibility of strange local customs that 'outsiders don't understand', which might create a habit of hostility to outsiders. Hostility can vary from a sullen disposition and a practice of giving vague or misleading answers to questions – perhaps even a refusal to serve outsiders in the local pub or shop – to outright refusing to deal with outsiders. In more remote or underdeveloped areas this might even include direct hostility of an armed and violent form. Operatives might be confronted with angry locals armed with shotguns, spears or whatever else is common in the area, especially if they are poking into things that are not their business.

Cities provide Our Other Enemy with places to hide, but so too does the countryside. Far away from official scrutiny, tied to older orders of life and older beliefs, and often incestuous in both the literal and figurative sense, the rural parts of the world are a hotbed for strange activity. Such cattle cells might be even more difficult to root out as they are protected by the suspicions of the locales towards any outsiders. In fact, an entire community might be part of the plot. When operating in rural areas, trust no one. -N

UNDERSTANDING THE LOCALS

Even if an investigator is not trying to pass themselves off as a local, they may still need to understand those around are them. If the investigator is trying to communicate with someone who speaks in a dialect or has an impenetrable accent, the Keeper should set the difficulty of the Other Language roll as Hard.

One of the main obstacles – or hazards – in the countryside is wildlife. Some of these are directly dangerous but others create a subtler problem. For example, operatives would naturally be cautious if there are dogs around – whether guard dogs or working animals – but other animals can readily give away an intruder. Geese are kept as guard animals in some cultures, and they have a tendency to make a great deal of noise and commotion if disturbed.

Wild birds can give away an operative's position by taking flight. A town-dweller might think nothing of seeing a handful of birds suddenly fly up into a nearby tree, but to someone used to living in the countryside this indicates that something – probably a predator – has disturbed them. This also draws attention to the location of the disturbance. Other animals, even docile cattle, may react to a stranger's presence by becoming agitated or by approaching in search of food.

NAVIGATING THE COUNTRYSIDE

While briefings, maps and compasses can help, it is all too easy to get lost in unfamiliar countryside. The Keeper should ask for a Navigate roll if failure could lead to interesting consequences. This may include stumbling across an enclave of locals, up to no good, or falling behind on the objective, forcing the investigators to take dangerous risks in making up lost time. If the investigators are travelling through countryside in the dark, or in bad weather, the Keeper may ask for a Hard Navigate roll due to decreased visibility.

Investigators spending significant time travelling through rural or remote areas may also be required to make a roll against the Survival specialisation appropriate to the environment. This is especially appropriate if the investigators have limited supplies or if the landscape is especially hostile.

You know all those old tales about witches and warlocks having animals under their control, familiars and the like? There might be some truth to them, or maybe it is just

my imagination. Still, when I am in the countryside and see all those animals, especially the birds, I can't help but feel they are watching me. - Rodriquez

Darkness in the countryside can present an easily underestimated hazard. On an overcast night in the countryside it can be virtually impossible to see where you are putting your feet, let alone any distance. Operatives must be prepared for this situation and perhaps carry a light source or else avoid being caught outside after dark.

OPERATING IN URBAN ENVIRONMENTS

The urban environment is better suited to most field operations than the countryside. However, there are certain considerations that need to be borne in mind when operating in the urban environment.

Wherever there are people gathered in one place, there is conflict. Rival criminal organisations and street gangs, or even just local drunks who resent a newcomer in 'their' bar, can all pose a hazard to the unwary operative. Other forms of conflict can be subtler but equally as dangerous; a housing dispute or a union on strike can change the conditions in a neighbourhood to the point of endangering operatives or preventing certain activities.

Operatives must be aware of social conditions. Obvious errors include attempting operations in an area repeatedly raided by police to break up gang activity, or having operations disrupted by local thieves.

 Our Other Enemy can be found in all parts of a city, from the seedy warrens of the poor to the gleaming halls of the rich and powerful. However, the madness and insanity of servants tends to drive those who pursue less-than-wholesome interests into the gutters.

This means you are more likely to be operating in areas prone to crime, as well as ethnic, racial and class violence. Keep a check on any prejudices you might have, and keep in mind that others will not be doing the same. -N

 You do not want to be caught in a race riot while hunting down a pack of cemetery creepers. - Miller

People are the main resource to be exploited in a city. If the operative can befriend someone they may be willing to offer help with trivial errands, reducing the amount of exposure the operative faces and the amount of challenge their cover identity meets. Money is more important to an operation in the urban environment; at the very least, it will be much easier to find someone who can be bribed, or a necessary item for sale.

Whatever the local means of exchange, 'hard currency' is popular – though possibly illegal – in many areas. Hard currency is money that is stable and will retain its value, such as pound sterling and US dollars, which tend to be vastly more stable than many Third World currencies. Even where local money does not become wildly devalued overnight, Western currencies are often prized very highly. However, the authorities tend to watch for those using hard currency either from a law enforcement perspective or out of corrupt self-interest.

Care must be taken when undertaking what is termed 'big-budget espionage'. Money can be a short-term solution to problems, but it is not a bludgeon that can be used with impunity. Trying to buy people and services can attract far much attention; word travels fast in the urban environment.

The urban world is also very cluttered. What separates places is not so much the distance between them as the time and effort required to get from one to the other. Bridges and other river crossings are ideal places for checkpoints or observers, while railway stations are obvious security points.

Old cities often have crooked streets that do not lead where they look like they might, or unexpected dead ends where an area has been redeveloped. An operative can easily lose their bearings in an unfamiliar area, derailing the timings on a sensitive operation.

Light is another important consideration. Few areas are completely dark, and many are too well lit to allow stealthy operations. This can work both ways: some light is necessary for operations at night, whilst too much makes it difficult to avoid detection.

As a rule, operatives in an urban area do better to hide in plain sight, disguising themselves as someone with legitimate business in the area, rather than trying to avoid detection altogether. Even if the target of the operation is somewhere conducive to stealth, transit to and from that area will probably have to cross populated, well-lit areas and due consideration to appearance should be given.

MOBILITY, INFILTRATION AND EXFILTRATION

Much of the time an operative's methods of mobility will be dictated not so much by efficiency as what will attract the least amount of notice. Patience is an essential virtue in intelligence work; no matter how urgent the situation, little is gained by attracting attention. Operatives may have to amble when they want to rush, or take a roundabout route rather than climbing over a fence and proceeding directly to the target location.

Similarly, means of mobility must tie in with an operative's cover identity. Air travel is expensive, and beyond the means of many working-class people. If the operative's cover identity would not be able to afford to fly then they cannot unless they adopt a different persona for the journey, and that carries with it a whole new set of risks.

At times fairly basic means of transport are more effective than others. In a traffic-choked city it may be more efficient to use a bicycle or moped than an executive saloon. Again, cover identity will determine whether this is appropriate.

Whatever means of transportation are used, for most operations there are distinct phases of mobility: approach, infiltration and exfiltration. The approach to the target area should be made as efficiently as possible. It is possible to circumvent the question of whether the transport fits with the operative's cover identity by remaining out of sight in the back of a van or hiding in the footwell of a car, but it will then be necessary to avoid being seen getting into and out of the vehicle.

INFILTRATION

Approach movement ends at the mission ready point, which will usually be well short of any heavily secured area. From this point onward, the operatives are engaged in infiltration. Infiltration by stealth requires an indirect approach, possibly accompanied by the removal of guards and sentries. A stealthy infiltration is usually made on foot, which allows speed to be varied according to circumstances.

Fast movement can be noisy and makes early detection of hazards difficult, but constantly creeping along not only takes a long time but can wear down the patience of operatives who might pick exactly the wrong moment to start advancing at a faster pace. A suitable balance must be struck, with occasional pauses to assess the situation and observe the lay of the land ahead.

A deceptive infiltration has entirely different speed requirements. Operatives must move at a pace that will not attract suspicion. Thus an operative trying to mingle with a crowd headed towards a sporting or music event must move with the flow of people; one who is approaching a mansion pretending to be a guest at a function cannot be seen to be in too much of a hurry. Obviously, a deceptive infiltration also requires a disguise or cover identity and the ability to get past any security without raising the alarm or causing mayhem.

It may be possible to build 'dashes' into an infiltration wherever the operative can be sure they will not be observed. However, a dinner guest who arrives sweaty or dishevelled will attract attention, so fast movement must be used judiciously. Infiltration takes as long as it takes.

The entire infiltration phase of an operation can be replaced with a reckless charge under some circumstances. It may be possible to launch an assault from a position close to the target if it is a remote area or has poor sight lines, or for operatives to blatantly drive up to the gates and shoot their way in. This is generally inadvisable, but it is occasionally effective and sometimes is the only possible approach. However, choosing to make an assault rather than an infiltration should be a last resort.

Movement during the active phase of the mission might be stealthy, deceptive or aggressive depending on circumstances. Often a combination of the three can be used. For example a disguised operative might walk right past one security checkpoint, sneak through an area that guests are not supposed to enter then dash to the objective when the opportunity arises. They might then explain their presence using deception and allow themselves to be escorted back to the party with important documents in their pocket. Creativity and good judgement are necessary under such complex circumstances.

CALLING FOR ROLLS DURING OPERATIONS

 The Keeper must resist the temptation to call for too many rolls when investigators are on missions. Always remember that the investigators are trained professionals, usually with field experience. They should not fail routine activities. Rolls should only be called for when they face active resistance, are working from faulty intelligence or circumstances have forced them to improvise.

If rolls are required, consider using combined rolls rather than a string of skill checks. Breaking into a building may require Stealth and Locksmith; calling for separate rolls against both lowers the chances of the investigator succeeding. There may be occasions where this is appropriate, such as when the investigators are facing active opposition, but most of the time it will simply devalue the abilities of skilled characters. Similarly, when investigators are working in a team, don't ask every player to make the same skill roll. For Stealth rolls, for example, it may be appropriate to ask for a roll for the investigator with the highest skill when they are leading the rest of the team. Under less controlled circumstances, the person with the lowest skill should make the roll for the group instead.

EXFILTRATION

Exfiltration is the opposite of infiltration, and subject to similar considerations. In some circumstances, 'withdrawal' might be a better term than exfiltration, especially if an operation has 'gone loud'. However, exfiltration or 'exfil'

covers all methods of leaving the operational area. A rapid withdrawal, perhaps accompanied by gunfire and pursuit, is not the ideal ending to an operation but may be the only option. However, it is far better to stealthily slip out again or walk out the front door after bidding the target a fond goodnight than to frantically try to break contact with pursuers.

To this end, one critical decision about exfiltration is when to begin. If an operation has been noisy or bodies have been left lying around, getting out as soon and as quickly as possible seems to be the best option. However, even then it may be possible to dissemble through the inevitable questions and leave later with cover identity still intact. This requires a steady nerve and a cast-iron cover, however.

Exfiltration may be by the same means as infiltration, or could take an entirely different approach. Operatives have been known to obtain a guard's equipment and clothing to join a pursuit, slipping away at some suitable juncture.

One particularly daring strategy is to remain in the target location but misdirect its security personnel into going outside to look for the operative. This can clear the way to a secondary objective, or even the primary objective if the alert was triggered by some other circumstance.

More commonly, the operative must decide whether to leave immediately after the operation is carried out or to remain on site and try to allay suspicion. Once the decision to leave is made then stealth or deception – or both – are used to get out of the immediate operational vicinity and to break contact with any pursuers or observers. Final withdrawal might be made using a vehicle left for the purpose, but this risks discovery or even an ambush.

Alternatively, an exfiltration team (or just a single operative) will meet the operational team with whatever is needed to get completely out of the area. This will usually include a vehicle of some kind, but might also include changes of clothing, supplies, documents and anything else the operation team might require. A secondary exfiltration point should be agreed beforehand, and possibly a backup plan if that, too, is compromised.

Getting out after a mission is every bit as important as getting in, and not only from the point of view of operative survival. Ideally, the operative's cover remains intact after an operation, but at the very least the opposition should not be able to deduce too much from how the operative went about carrying out the mission.

By way of example, there are two very different approaches to a task as simple as stealing a target's wallet. One option involves kicking his front door in, hurling flashbangs and concussion grenades around his living room and shooting his dog. Furniture is overturned, the target is roughed up and the house is set on fire before the operatives leave with the wallet. Alternatively, one day the owner realises that he cannot find his wallet, but has no idea what has happened to it nor when he last saw it. He is not even sure what was in it, so when he finds it again he is not sure if anything is missing or if his money has been replaced with counterfeit notes. Or perhaps the contents of the wallet are examined and copied, but the wallet then replaced, the owner none the wiser.

The first option is relatively easy to set up using a brute force approach, but the victim will be on the alert thereafter. A stealthy approach to infiltration followed by a rapid withdrawal with the wallet obtains the wallet and its contents, but again the victim will know something has occurred. The best approach is one where the victim never even realises that anything has happened, so that if it later turns out that the dog must be killed or the house set on fire there is no high alert status to make this more difficult.

Infiltration is vital to completing the mission at hand, but exfiltration is equally important to avoid making future operations that much harder. It also helps keep our operatives alive and in the game, so must not be neglected. It is far too easy to think in terms only of the objective; good intelligence work is always conducted with an eye to the future.

MOVEMENT IN THE FACE OF THE ENEMY

If the operative must move around in an area close to the enemy, the best choice is probably deception; the operative goes about his business openly under some sort of cover. It is generally easier to walk up to a gate carrying a delivery of flowers or bread than it is to creep through the undergrowth and try to slip through.

 Our Other Enemy needs to remain as covert in their actions and membership as we do. They do not want to attract the official gaze, and one fine way to get into their lairs is to pose as a minor public officer. Law enforcement is too threatening, but the electric and water meters still need to be read, buildings still get inspected, and most nations run a census of some kind. – Rodriguez

If deception is used, the operative will have to talk their way into the target locality. This means having a good cover story for the infiltration and suitable props to support it, as well as the ability to lie convincingly. It helps if the victims of the deception are predisposed to believe the cover story; a hurriedly concocted tale about a last-minute call to examine a noisy electrical generator is less believable than yet another delivery of food and wine for the target's upcoming party.

A certain amount of research and information gathering is necessary when planning any mission, and some of this should be directed at the habits of the target and their security staff. If certain local firms are used for deliveries and their vans are waved through security without inspection, this is the ideal means of infiltration. If the target has very fixed habits then any deviation from the usual timings and methods will arouse suspicion that will not be allayed by any amount of persuasion.

 I once posed as a health inspector to get into a café run as a front by a cell. Got a good look at their layout and numbers, cited them for a few violations, and even picked up a small bribe to look the other way. – Miller

Similar comments apply to evading capture by patrols in the countryside. The best way to break contact with pursuit or to slip past a patrol is to have them discount the operative as harmless. A patrol searching for a suspected infiltrator might approach a gentleman fishing by the river to ask if he has seen anything or advise him to leave the area. They may suspect that this is the infiltrator but if their suspicions can be allayed with a well-delivered cover story the infiltrator has gone one better than bypassing this patrol – he has made them essentially blind to his presence.

If deception is not possible then it is necessary to hide or sneak. The operative must be mindful of colours, shapes and movement. For example, if an operative is climbing over a fence and finds themselves illuminated, movement will draw the eye in a way that a static shape will not. An operative standing by a fence is obvious; one who is lying along a fence rail so that the operative's body blends into the rail's shape much less so. Since the observer's eye expects to see a long shape at that point, it may not discern the human figure against the expected shape of the fence.

The shape of the human head or face is very distinctive and will draw attention if it is spotted somewhere unexpected. The same goes for anything straight, such as a rifle barrel, since straight lines do not occur in nature. Covering straight objects in netting or putting a sack over them can greatly assist in maintaining a covert posture. However, this presupposes that the item does not stand out because it is metallic or of a colour that makes it very obvious to an observer.

Dark colours are generally harder to make out than light ones, especially at night. However, black tends to be 'too dark' and dark grey, blue or green are better choices for night-time concealment. If colours are used for camouflage, they must match the local foliage or other colours. Green and brown disruptive patterns stand out against brickwork, and even a slight variation in colour can stand out on the edge of a forest.

Movement, especially fast or regular movement, is another giveaway. The human eye is better at spotting a stationary object that starts to move than one that is already in motion, which is one reason that the 'sniper crawl' works. Under the right conditions it is possible to crawl across fairly open ground, under observation, for very long distances without being spotted.

Military snipers – albeit exceptional ones – have been known to crawl for the better part of a mile to reach a firing position, shoot a key enemy figure and then creep away again without being seen. However, this requires incredible endurance and patience, since covering a mile at this pace might take an entire day or even more.

The rule for stealthy movement in the face of the enemy is 'low and slow', with lower tending to equate to slower. When under good cover or unobserved the operative can move quickly in an upright posture, dropping into a crouch when cover is not so good or the opposition is close. Crawling on all fours is tiring and slow, but a 'flat crawl' or 'sniper crawl' is even more exhausting. In this posture the operative is flat to the ground, moving by pushing themselves with the feet and pulling with their arms without bending limbs or lifting their body off the ground.

With good camouflage or in darkness, an operative moving like this is virtually impossible to spot unless the enemy is right on top of them... and even then they can be missed if they freeze in place.

SPOT RULES FOR SNIPER CRAWLS

 A lengthy sniper crawl is as much a matter of physical endurance and mental discipline as it is of stealthiness. An investigator attempting such a crawl should make a combined roll against CON, POW and Stealth to represent this. Failure does not necessarily mean that the sniper is spotted, but that their stamina or resolve is failing. The investigator may attempt to drive themselves on by pushing the roll, but this time failure will mean discovery or any other consequence the Keeper deems appropriate.

SPECIAL FORMS OF MOVEMENT

Special forms of movement may also be used by operatives when required. These include rappelling out of a helicopter, abseiling down a building or cliff, and swimming to the target. Rappelling and similar fast-rope techniques are mainly used by assault troops, but operatives may be required to use this skill for a fast insertion. For example, a helicopter ostensibly carrying out an innocent mission might drop off an operative or a team along the way. If there is nowhere to land, or if landing might be observed, then fast-rope techniques are useful.

Spot Rules for Rappelling

Unless an investigator is under time pressure or threat, there is no need for a roll to rappel down a rope. If the circumstances are fraught or dangerous, the Keeper may ask for a DEX roll. Failure may indicate that the process is taking long enough to put the investigator at risk. The player may call for a second, pushed roll, with the Keeper setting consequences such as becoming entangled or taking damage from falling or enemy fire.

Spot Rules for Parachuting

On rare occasions, investigators may have to parachute into hostile territory to perform covert actions or, in worst-case scenarios, parachute from a plane that is in the process of crashing. The basics of parachuting can be taught relatively quickly, and do not require specific training, though mastery can be a skill of its own (see below).

Given that most aeroplanes are likely to be flying hundreds of metres above ground level, a fall without a parachute is a near certain fatality. The *Other Damage* table on pg. 124 of the *Call of Cthulhu rulebook* would place such a fall in the "splat" category, inflicting 8D10 of damage; even halving this with a successful Jump roll is unlikely to lead to a happy outcome. Under routine conditions, the Keeper should not call for a roll when trained or experienced investigators make a parachute jump. If the conditions are dangerous, such as coming in under enemy fire, executing a LALO jump or parachuting from an aeroplane that is out of control, use the following rules.

When parachuting under such circumstances, the investigator must pass a DEX roll with two bonus dice. Success means that the character is free and clear of the aircraft and has pulled the ripcord for the parachute without difficulty. If this roll is failed, this means that the parachute is tangled with the aeroplane or the investigator is disorientated and falling incorrectly. The investigator may attempt a DEX roll with a bonus die to free the chute or to right themselves.

If the second roll is also a failure, this means the chute is tangled or was improperly deployed. All hope is not lost! The investigator can use their reserve chute, requiring a Regular DEX roll. If that last-ditch roll is also a failure, the investigator falls, taking 8D6 damage (4D6 if the investigator passes a Jump roll) from the fall and likely meets an untimely end. If the last roll is a success, the reserve chute opens and the parachuting investigator must make a Jump roll land properly with. Failing the Jump roll causes 1D6 points of damage, or 1D10 if the roll is a fumble.

If for some reason the investigator is parachuting without any training or experience, the Keeper may require a combined INT and DEX roll for the investigator to be able work out how to scramble into the chute. Getting out of an aeroplane in an uncontrolled jump (such as a plane spiralling towards the ground) may require a Jump or Dodge roll.

Any physical action (combat skills, Dodge, Throw or similar) attempted while parachuting will require a Hard roll.

Finding an ideal spot to land might require a Spot Hidden roll, and landing without being spotted (or quickly gathering and concealing the parachute and harness) requires a Stealth roll. Ideally, the landing is in an open field, airstrip or cleared area, away from trees. If the investigator is forced to land among trees, the keeper should require a DEX or Luck roll to avoid the parachute being tangled and caught. If the chute is caught, the investigator must make a successful Climb or Jump roll to get disentangled from the parachute cords without taking damage. If this roll is unsuccessful, the investigator may take damage from the fall as per the normal falling rules.

Other means of using aircraft for an insertion tend to be rather specialised but are sometimes the only way to get an operative into an area quickly. Parachuting and landings by light aircraft were used with success by SOE during World War Two and remain useful but have since been augmented by special techniques. These include HALO (High Altitude/Low Opening) jumps, whereby the operative makes a long free fall from an altitude so high that oxygen is required, opening the parachute very late to avoid detection.

LALO (Low Altitude/Low Opening) is an even more extreme technique. In this method, an aircraft such as a C-130 Hercules flies very low and delivers operatives or troops by suddenly entering a near-vertical climb so that the personnel essentially fall out of the open cargo ramp at the rear. Static lines automatically open their parachutes immediately, but since the delivery altitude is just a few hundred feet a LALO jump can only be made over water – and even then the impact is hard.

A parachute and associated equipment is a dead giveaway that personnel or materiel have been delivered to an area, so operatives who have landed or received equipment need to hide the chutes as quickly as possible and then leave the area. A hard-learned rule developed by SOE during World War Two is that operatives should never, under any circumstances, return to the site of a parachute insertion. Anything that is hidden there is lost once the operative leaves the area.

Insertion from water can be carried out using boats, swimming or more exotic means. Certain submarines are equipped to deliver divers off an enemy coast, often with propulsion aids to permit them to carry more equipment or transit further without tiring. Insertion can be direct to shore but rivers and inlets offer a chance to bypass the coast to some extent. Advanced equipment such as propulsion units should be returned to the parent vessel by a retrieval team, whereas more basic items such as swim fins can be concealed in the manner of a parachute. Similar comments apply as for parachutes; operatives cannot return to the site of concealed swimming equipment unless it has been secured by an exfiltration team.

Abseiling is used to get down a vertical or near-vertical surface from above. It allows an indirect approach to a target area that might not be detected, but requires that equipment be transported to the start point and left there. Anyone caught on a rope is very vulnerable, so abseiling should be used with caution. It is also rather difficult to get back up a rope quickly, so an abseil is usually considered a one-way option with exfiltration by some other means.

SPOT RULES FOR ABSEILING

Unless an investigator is under time pressure or threat, there is no need for a roll to abseil down a surface safely. If the circumstances are fraught or dangerous, the Keeper may ask for a DEX roll. If the investigator is trying to operate quietly, this may be combined with a Stealth roll.

If the investigator fails this roll, they have become temporarily stuck. A second, pushed roll is required to continue, with the Keeper setting consequences for failure that may include discovery, becoming stuck or falling, with resultant damage.

BREAKING AND ENTERING

Missions requiring breaking into a building are often referred to as 'black bag' operations. Breaking and entering is never the goal of the mission; it is something that is necessary to facilitate the desired outcome. However, no black bag operation should ever be considered trivial; something as simple as a dead bolt can derail an entire mission.

Most operatives have at least some training in lock picking and similar means of bypassing security, but picking a lock can take time even for the most skilled of operatives. There is always a risk of discovery, and since these are rather obvious 'negative' activities it will be hard to come up with a plausible reason for doing so. The best that the would-be burglar can hope for is to be taken for a criminal or perhaps an unethical journalist, rather than an intelligence operative.

Mechanical locks are not usually very complex and can be picked with simple tools, but there are alternatives. Often the device itself can be operated without unlocking it, by slipping a thin object though the space between door and frame. Combination locks cannot be picked in the same manner as mechanical ones but are often susceptible to the same weaknesses. A deadbolt is impervious to this treatment, however, remaining firmly engaged with the door frame unless manually or electrically withdrawn. This cannot be done from outside the door.

When selecting an entry point, assuming that stealth is desirable, an operatives should work on a lowest likelihood of discovery basis rather than the easiest lock to pick or the most convenient entry point. This is especially true if physical damage to the door or window is necessary to open it. Many windows are poorly secured and can be forced without difficulty, but this may make noise or cause damage. Choosing the right entry point greatly reduces the chance of discovery.

If it is not possible to gain entry by quietly picking a lock or forcing a poorly secured window, noisier methods might be required. Breaking a pane of glass in a door may give access to a key or dead bolt on the inside, but will make a noise. This can be reduced if the operative pushes the glass out of place rather than just smashing through it, especially if a small pane can be pushed from one corner and removed intact. Noise can also be covered by sounds coming from elsewhere, though obviously broken glass or a missing pane may well be spotted.

Operatives can abandon any attempt to remain covert and smash their way through doors or windows. The 'fireman's key' (a heavy kick delivered to the door) is quick but noisy, and lighter doors can be shoulder-charged. For secure doors, the best option may be to shoot out the hinges or bolts with a shotgun.

Alarms and other security systems – including lethal ones – are usually keyed to entry points and passageways. The simplest sound an alarm when a fence is cut or a door is opened. These can often be bypassed by running a connector (a wire) between points on each side of the area to be cut or the circuit that will be broken by opening the door, ensuring that current continues to flow.

 Fair warning, some of our foes employ unnatural security measures that put even the most ferocious Doberman to shame. -N

However, the best way to bypass security systems of this sort is to make use of natural and routine breaks in the system, or to get the operators to bypass the system themselves. If a door is routinely opened to let a sentry make their rounds, then this can be exploited by an operative moving into the building. Alarms are sometimes set off by accident or technical malfunction, and will often be reset without being checked if this is a frequent nuisance.

Operatives can exploit this by deliberately setting off the alarm at intervals over a few days. After a while the operators will stop rushing out to see what has caused the alert and will simply reset the 'malfunctioning' system.

Natural security systems such as guard dogs can be spoofed in a similar way, by getting them to raise an alarm so often that they are discounted. However, there is an additional risk if the guards' response is to release the dogs. As an alternative, dogs can be given food, contentedly causing them to watch intruders without barking. Food can also be drugged or poisoned, or guard animals can also be shot with a suppressed handgun: the Smith & Wesson Model 23 'Hush Puppy' got its nickname from its use for this purpose by US Special Forces teams in Vietnam (see *World War Cthulhu: Cold War*, pg. 151).

As with any situation that leaves evidence lying around, shooting or drugging a guard dog starts the 'discovery clock' ticking. If robust methods are used to bypass security or to force an entry the operation should remain covert if possible but needs to move to a 'fast and quiet' approach rather than a more time-consuming stealthy posture. The unknown amount of time before the intrusion is discovered must be used to best effect, which means that greater risks are justifiable in order to get further in or even to complete the mission before the alert is sounded.

Wherever possible, operatives should take advantage of the enemy's routine or holes in his security coverage, and also of weak points such as predictable shift changes or unimaginative patrol schedules. The most difficult part of an infiltration should be timed to coincide with the lowest alert on the part of the security force. This is typically entry to a building through the main secured obstacle – its outside doors and windows – but might instead be some mission-critical transition through an area that is normally well patrolled.

As with most other field operations, time is a critical factor when entering a secured area, but this does not equate to haste. Good timing and expert use of variances in speed may be critical. For example it may be necessary to rush across a courtyard while the guards are distracted, then wait for several minutes for a shift change before attempting to pick the lock on the chosen entry point. Judging the right moment is much vital, and any technical task such as lock picking must be completed in a quick but unhurried manner.

Likewise, it may be necessary to make the decision to abandon an attempt to pick a given lock or force a window and withdraw or seek another way in. This must be finely judged, as must the decision to resort to forcing an entry rather than opening a door and slipping inside. Operatives must not become fixated on one method; there are times when the fireman's key is more appropriate than the clever use of a black bag. However, as always, the rule is that once noise is made or damage is done, there may be little to gain from remaining covert.

Operatives should always be willing to abandon a mission and make another attempt if this is a better option. A failed entry will alert the enemy, and even a successful one may be counterproductive if it is detected. These matters should have been considered when the mission was planned, enabling operatives to make intelligent decisions based on the circumstances around them.

Nobody likes to report an aborted mission, but sometimes this is the best decision. If so, it is the operative's duty to withdraw and accept the failure rather than bludgeoning through for the sake of ego or a perfect operational record.

Bollocks to the train, train.
Buy or rent a car, plenty of room to manoeuvre and get away if you have to. Plenty, plenty of places to hide. Hide and read.
No conductors looking at you and knowing, knowing.

Easier to hide the body, though on a train you could just toss, toss it. - Stanton

CHAPTER FOUR

SURVEILLANCE AND INTELLIGENCE GATHERING

SURVEILLANCE AND
·INTELLIGENCE GATHERING·

Information gathering is the most important activity carried out by an intelligence operative. It is the primary purpose of many missions and is necessary to every mission. For every mission that has complete and accurate information already in place at the planning stage, there is another mission mounted to gather it in the first place.

It is worth noting that in our line of work anyone who thinks they have complete and accurate information is overdue for retirement; there is no such thing. Data can look good but be incomplete, inaccurate or just flat-out wrong. An essential part of preparing any mission is to corroborate, cross-check and verify as much of the available information as possible.

Information gathering by operatives and assets is termed 'Human Intelligence' (HUMINT) and can take three main forms. Tertiary information gathering makes use of sources such as newspapers, tourist maps and similar commonly available items. The operative has no control over the accuracy of information gained from such sources, but they can be a useful means of getting bulk data or basic information for little effort and virtually no risk.

You might be tempted to dismiss tertiary sources of information; such would be a foolish thing to do. You will not find one article or other item that points out the existence of Our Other Enemy, but the entire picture might be found in pieces. The local newspaper story about missing cats, another story about a break in at a warehouse, and a third piece of gossip concerning a brawl at the docks might all be parts of a larger picture. -N

Secondary information gathering is based on reports made by assets run by the operative or informants who might be paid or otherwise induced to provide data. It may be that an asset who is well placed can get data that an operative cannot. Secondary information gathering is not always reliable; an asset could make mistakes or invent details for their own reasons. They might give outright false or misleading information or leave out part of the truth if it suits their agenda.

Secondary data must be treated with some suspicion but it is a means of obtaining intelligence for relatively little risk.

Primary intelligence gathering is undertaken by the operative directly. This is riskier than employing an asset or buying a newspaper. Regardless of the danger level, primary information gathering allows the operative to be sure that what is reported is what is seen. Whilst the best data usually comes from complex and well-executed missions, much of the information gathered by operatives comes from mundane activities that can be generally grouped as surveillance and observation. We draw a distinction between the two for convenience more than anything else; the principles are the same for both.

First thing I do when in a new city is pick up one of each of the local newspapers. Even grab up the wild hippie rags, those freaks sometimes have something of value. Really, the whole counter-culture thing is like bait for Our Other Enemy. - Miller

Observation is little more than 'keeping your eyes open' and gathering information from whatever mundane sources are available. It does not require any real covert activity, other than the routine maintenance of a cover identity or disguise. Observation can take the form of buying and reading a newspaper or counting the trucks that go past whilst eating lunch at a restaurant.

Observation is unlikely to garner any deep secrets unless the opposition slips up, but it allows a picture to be built of the general situation and some of the specifics. It is easy to forget about the wealth of information that can be obtained by routine observation, but it is extremely important. Observation of this sort generally creates a huge volume of low-value information, which must be collated and analysed.

This takes time and a considerable amount of effort, and is often considered a waste of time.

This impression is incorrect; low-value data often has important information concealed within it, and even if it does not the general picture it provides can be used to give context to more specific pieces of information. These specific data items are often obtained by targeted surveillance of a person or place; without general observation we might not know where to look.

INFORMATION GATHERING

The Keeper should always look for ways to reward thorough planning. If the investigators have carefully and successfully researched a potential recruit's life before approaching her, they should gain one or two bonus dice on any interpersonal skill rolls made while convincing the agent to work for them. Similarly, detailed knowledge of a target's normal movements may give a bonus on rolls made to assassinate him, and thorough surveillance of a facility should afford a bonus on roll to infiltrate it.

Of course, luck also plays a role. All that detailed information gathering may be for naught if your target cancels plans due to sickness, or the facility is subject to a surprise audit on the day of the mission. The Keeper may call for a group Luck roll to determine if anything unexpected has changed.

SURVEILLANCE

Surveillance is the business of covertly watching a person or place, or listening to what is happening there. It differs from observation in that the methods used are 'sneaky'. Surveillance can be carried out by technical means such as a listening device, but it still has to be put in place. Likewise, direct surveillance by personnel must be covert, requiring either concealment, disguise, or both. Where technical aids are required, such as binoculars or a camera, the task of keeping surveillance covert becomes much more difficult.

A key factor is the necessity of balancing risk to potential reward. It is rare that any given piece of surveillance work justifies exposing operatives to significant risks, and quite often there will be places where the subject cannot be kept under observation. If the opposition have done a good job of securing an area or have robust security procedures it may be necessary to abandon surveillance at a certain point and pick up the subject again when they leave the secured area.

By way of example, the enemy might have their own counter-surveillance personnel tailing the subject or sweeping the area around his route. These personnel will know what makes a good observation point and will be highly suspicious of anyone they encounter in such an area even if there is no overt activity. This sort of security arrangement is manpower-intensive and is rarely encountered other than for very important individuals working on highly sensitive projects.

Our Other Enemy often possesses senses or esoteric means of observation we have little understanding of. Keep this in mind when setting up your surveillance operation. Your blind might be perfectly hidden from mundane detection and secure against electromagnetic detection, but you still might be caught out by something that can 'see' between walls or even possess precognitive abilities. Always, always keep two or more escape options open. -N

The best form of surveillance is to place an operative somewhere they can observe the subject on a long-term basis, such as working in a bar the subject spends a lot of time in, or insinuating someone into their workplace. It is occasionally possible to position someone at the centre of the subject's life by means of a friendship, romantic attachment or business arrangement engineered by the operatives. More commonly, an operative can be positioned or an asset obtained somewhere loosely connected with the subject's routine, giving a patchier coverage for less effort.

If it is not possible to attach someone to the target or their entourage, more conventional surveillance operations are necessary. Surveillance can be static or mobile; often an operation will be a bit of both. Static surveillance is easier to carry out than mobile, and can be performed either using concealment or disguise.

Concealment can be quite basic, such as sitting in a car or using bushes for cover. If access to buildings is possible then a suitable window makes an excellent vantage point. Few people look above their eye height, so unless the operatives make movements close to the window that will draw the eye then they will remain concealed. Similarly, rooftops can be used for 'concealed' surveillance even if the operatives are not actually hidden. Unless they give themselves away, they are not likely to be spotted except by trained counter-surveillance personnel. As always, a low profile and a lack of sudden or large movements will allow the operatives to remain covert.

specific disguise, such as posing as workmen or handing out advertising flyers, but more commonly the disguise takes the form of a cover activity. Cover activities need not be complex; walking a dog or having lunch in a pavement cafe will suffice, but the key to disguising surveillance activity is for it to be immediately obvious what 'those people' are doing.

The last thing an operative needs is for a passer-by to wonder what they are up to. A cover activity that has to be explained is far less useful than one that is immediately obvious as innocuous. Two men in business suits having lunch whilst surrounded by briefcases and other business paraphernalia suggests 'business lunch'; it will be quickly forgotten by casual observers. Two men hanging around with no obvious purpose will cause passers-by to wonder what they are doing and perhaps remember them if questioned later.

One of the most significant threats to a surveillance operation is the possibility that passers-by may become involved. This can be as simple as someone demanding to know what the operatives are doing, and might happen for a variety of reasons. For example, the operatives might be confused with criminals, or mistaken for police or political enforcement agencies. Local gangs might also consider the operation to be an intrusion onto their 'turf'. Even if nothing serious happens, an operatives does not want to attract attention.

The main problem with using high vantage points is the difficulty in following if the subject moves on. An observation post of this sort must be set up well in advance, since the operatives need to reach their high position, and without attracting attention. The effort required to obtain high observation points is wasteful if the subject is only in view for a short time, so this method should only be considered if the subject is fixed in their routine or if the position offers a view of their home or workplace.

The behaviour of the subject can have consequences for the operatives. A subject who annoys people creates a hostile atmosphere in which the operatives have to work. They may receive the backlash from whatever the subject did, especially if people think they are connected. This is possible if the operatives stand out in any way.

Surveillance operatives are far less likely to run into problems if they look like they belong in the area or are engaged in some innocuous activity. However important the surveillance operation may be, operatives must not fixate upon the mission to the point where they start to stand out, or else the mission is likely to fail. Often there is a choice to be made between good but risky surveillance and patchier but more covert operations; in most cases covert is the default choice.

Mobile Surveillance and Counter-Surveillance

Sometimes a location rather than a person is the subject of such a stakeout. It may be necessary to watch a building or other location for an extended period during which virtually nothing happens. Operatives need to remain alert enough

Selecting a Suitable Vantage Point

 Identifying a suitable vantage point for surveillance calls for a combined Stealth and Tradecraft roll. If the investigator does not have time to scope the area out properly ahead of time, the Keeper may also call for a Luck roll for there to be an accessible vantage point.

Disguise in the context of surveillance means that the operatives are in plain sight, and are using some means of making their activities seem innocuous. This might require a

to react if the situation changes or of they are 'made', but for the most part they will simply spend long hours sitting around. Negative information can sometimes be useful, such as when a target's suspected location can be narrowed down by finding out where they are not. Most stakeouts are boring – not at all like the glamorous lives of fictional spies.

Staying Alert During Stakeouts

 If an investigator stakes out a location for an extended period of time, the Keeper should call for a combined CON and POW roll to determine if they manage to stay alert throughout. Failure results in any Spot Hidden or Listen rolls being made at a Hard difficulty level. The investigator may gain bonus dice on the CON/POW roll by splitting the surveillance with other team members or using stimulants to stay alert.

Mobile surveillance conducted on foot is a tricky business; using vehicles even more so. Often a semi-mobile method is employed, whereby the operatives drive or walk to a static observation point, then move on to another. This is generally much simpler than 'tailing' a subject on the move, but does require a certain amount of care.

Use of Vehicles

Using a car as a base for semi-mobile surveillance provides both mobility and concealment; few people will look into a car, so it may be possible to use binoculars or a camera in locations where they would otherwise be noticed in the open. It is important to select the vehicle carefully.

Cars should be nondescript and suited to the area they are working in. A beat-up family car will not stand out in some neighbourhoods where an executive saloon would be very obvious, and vice versa. Performance is far less important than appearance, though a vehicle must above all be reliable. It should be impossible or very difficult to trace back to the network.

As a rule, theft is not a good option for obtaining a vehicle; it may be reported, risking interference from the local police. Theft is useful as a short-term expedient but wherever possible vehicles should be obtained ahead of time and modified by changing their number plates and their colour.

A good option is to buy a vehicle privately for cash or from a dealer through a false identity. Offering a good (but not extravagant) price can reduce a seller's willingness to ask questions.

Care should be taken to find out if the car has a history; operatives have been known to drive around in vehicles hurriedly sold by criminals after being used in a robbery or body dump. Illegal or unroadworthy vehicles remain a viable option if the means exists to repair them and create a false identity. This is unlikely to be a capability that exists within a network, but some workshops may be willing to do this for a price if approached carefully. Contacts in a criminal organisation can often assist, but should never be trusted.

Assuming a suitable vehicle is available, using it is largely a matter of common sense. Operatives must be familiar with local traffic laws and the behaviour of road users. In many areas these are quite different concepts, and a vehicle scrupulously obeying traffic regulations that everyone else ignores will stand out just as much as one driving recklessly amongst sedate traffic. Operatives must not fixate so much on their surveillance task that they forget about basic driving skills.

Embassy cars with diplomatic plates should be avoided for most purposes. Diplomatic cars do have their uses, however. For example, this might be the only way to get an operative into a particular area. They can be dropped off somewhere secluded and picked up again when the car leaves. Alternatively the diplomatic car might be used to 'flush out' a response. Most sensitive and secret locations have a policy of advising personnel to not approach cars with diplomatic plates, but instead to respond in an indirect manner, usually by placing 'polite obstacles' in the way of any further forays. By observing the low-key response to a car going somewhere it should not, it may be possible to determine that the enemy has something concealed there.

Tailing a Subject

'Tailing' a subject follows similar principles whether on foot or in a vehicle. The operative must remain close enough to keep the subject in sight but proximity increases the risk of detection. It is sometimes necessary to hang back and lose sight of the subject from time to time, risking losing them completely in return for a reduced possibility of being spotted. If this is the case, a measure of educated guesswork is necessary to predict where the subject will go next and to reacquire them before they are out of sight too long. This is a risky strategy, but is sometimes the only way to avoid detection.

Tailing a person or vehicle requires quick wits in order to react to what the target does. If they start browsing through a market stall or pull over to buy a cup of coffee, the operative following must find a plausible reason to also stop, or must pass by and wait until the subject moves on again. This is a ways to spot a tail; a vehicle or person who matches your movements too closely is probably following you. The best way to deal with this is to have multiple operatives involved in a surveillance operation. If one is in a difficult position they can pass innocently by or turn off the road, leaving the subject to be picked up by another. However, this requires both the personnel and the coordination required to pull off the swap without being spotted.

Some subjects are blithely oblivious that they might be followed, which makes things much easier for the operative. However, with only very basic security precautions a subject can make themselves hard to tail without being spotted. If the operatives are 'made' then the subject may try to shake the tail. How overt they are might vary.

If the subject does not care if the operatives realise they have been 'made', they will probably make a sudden attempt to break contact by getting out of sight. They may simply flee, perhaps through an area that makes it difficult to follow. If they prefer the tail to think they have simply lost contact, the subject must be more subtle. Any fast movement will begin when out of sight of the operatives. The usual gambit is to pretend that nothing has been noticed then move briefly out of sight a few times before using one of these contact losses as an opportunity to get clear.

For example, the subject might turn several corners or move through an area with a lot of clutter, casually as if oblivious to the tail, then at a suitable juncture he will dash around another corner or otherwise put himself where the tail cannot find him when he attempts to reacquire contact. Entering a building then going out of a side door can work well, especially if the subject changes his appearance in the process; something as simple as putting on or removing a hat can make the subject difficult to reacquire once visual contact has been lost.

Attempts to lose a tail – covertly or otherwise – can become a battle of wits between the operative and their subject. Good counter-surveillance skills will also help an operative to spot the best opportunities for a subject to elude them and suggest where they might go. It is always risky to allow the subject to stay out of sight for more than a few seconds, but if the operative is reasonably sure the subject is about to attempt to break contact it may be necessary to take measures such as going around the other side of a building rather than following them directly. If the operative guesses correctly they will reacquire the subject when they think they have broken contact. If not, the operative's own action will cause the surveillance to fail. As with most other endeavours, a team of operatives can cover more options and provide some insurance against this sort of gambit.

Many subjects will routinely carry out 'dry cleaning' manoeuvres to shake off a tail even if they have not spotted one. Gambits such as using a different exit or rounding a corner and then suddenly dashing to another to get out of sight, as is the trick of taking four turns in the same direction when driving. If a car is still behind after the subject has driven in a circle, it is almost certainly a tail.

These gambits are routinely taught to government employees and military officers, and are often employed in a habitual and unimaginative manner. Someone who behaves like this is probably not a high-level security operative; the real experts are far subtler. However, even very basic dry cleaning can make a subject difficult to follow unless the operative can anticipate what they might do. The toughest subjects to follow are those who seem predictable, perhaps using routine, unimaginative tactics, and then suddenly do something completely unexpected. Being able to follow someone like this without being 'made' requires a combination of good skills and a certain amount of luck.

HANDLING MOBILE SURVEILLANCE

See the *Vehicular Surveillance* section on pg. 134 of *World War Cthulhu: Cold War* for guidelines about handling tails.

If an investigator picks up a tail, or is trying to follow a target who has realised that they are being tailed, and you want to play the cat-and-mouse game between pursuer and pursued in detail, it is possible to use a modified version of the chase rules from the *Call of Cthulhu* rulebook. These are usually subtler scenes than a normal chase, relying on cleverness and perception more than speed, so use Tradecraft rolls in place of DEX or Drive Auto. Manoeuvres might involve misdirection, ducking into crowds, doubling back and use of public transport.

ADDITIONAL CONSIDERATIONS

The worst-case scenario for surveillance work is not losing contact with the subject but instead being drawn into a trap. A surveillance team that is 'made' might be followed back to their safe house or swept up by a snatch team. A static observation point might be surrounded by hostile security personnel; a team on the move might be ambushed or confronted with overwhelming force. The fact that the operatives are tied to the movements of the subject creates a vulnerability that can be exploited by the opposition. Operatives must therefore remain vigilant in case they are under observation or being approached by hostiles. The option to break off surveillance and either return to innocuous activities or rapidly get out of the area must always be available. Exfiltration and escape routes must be open and ready at all times.

When using vehicles, whether for surveillance or to fulfil other transport requirements, operatives must keep in mind that their vehicle creates vulnerabilities as well as capabilities. It can be followed, watched, stolen or even rigged with explosives if the opposition is so inclined. Care must be taken when returning to a vehicle in case it is under observation; a few simple and unobtrusive measures can greatly reduce the chances of being caught by a rigged car.

PLANTING AND FINDING CAR BOMBS

See pg. 138 of *World War Cthulhu: Cold War* for details of planting and detecting car bombs.

Operatives should park on a slope where possible, making it difficult to place anything under the vehicle, and should approach it from a direction that allows an unobtrusive glance underneath. The 'dropped the keys' can be used but is obvious to those who know what to look for. Surveillance operatives should also watch for these actions on the part of a target. This will reveal if someone is security-aware or not.

If an observation point is used more than once it is possible for operatives to become highly complacent and treat it as 'home' or 'always safe' territory, when this is usually far from the case. An observation point must be observed before entering it every time it is used, and must be scrutinised for bugs, listening devices or evidence that someone else has been there. Otherwise there is a risk that the operatives will walk into a trap when they return to the observation post.

Equipment must not be left behind at an observation point if possible. It may attract thieves or be tampered with by enemy operatives, and most items will provoke interest from the opposing security services. Equipment that is left must be concealed or positioned where it will not attract notice.

Some items are sufficiently mundane that they can be left in the open or used as a means to conceal others, but no item connected specifically with espionage should ever be left where it can be found. Even if all that happens is theft by a light-fingered passer-by, the item might attract attention if sold or displayed, perhaps leading security personnel to realise that there are intelligence operatives active in the area.

USING TECHNICAL MEANS

Surveillance by technical means typically refers to the use of 'listening devices', which can intercept telephone or voice conversations. However, there are other means available, notably Signals Intelligence (SIGINT). This is the art of obtaining intelligence from signals of various sorts and can be subdivided into the fields of Communications Intelligence (COMINT) and Electronic Intelligence (ELINT).

ELINT is concerned with signals not directly used for communications, such as radar and similar emitters, as well as the general electromagnetic emissions from systems such as power transmission stations. ELINT can be used as a form of surveillance, in that it is often possible to track a vehicle or vessel emitting navigational or military radar signals. Much can be learned from analysis of these signals.

The fact that a radio is transmitting at all can provide useful information, especially when it is transmitting from a supposedly uninhabited place. Similarly, a military force can be kept under distant observation by detecting transmissions between sub-formations even if these cannot be understood by the surveillance operatives.

For the most part, ELINT methods are of limited use to surveillance operatives, as they only indicate that something is there rather than what it is doing or what is being said. An operative in the field is unlikely to have the equipment required to analyse radio transmissions in terms of strength and content, but since many radar and radio systems operate on known frequencies a certain amount of information can often be gleaned.

RADIO EAVESDROPPING

Radio communications in general are covered by the Signals skill, but this will only be useful if the transmissions are sent *en clair*. In the field, not even the Cryptography skill will help deal with encrypted transmissions. The only real hope is for the investigators to obtain the correct equipment to unscramble the broadcasts, which may be a mission objective in itself.

COMINT methods require the interception of a signal or transmission in an intelligible form. Phone tapping is a special case and is discussed below; for the most part we are concerned here with interception of radio transmissions. Most sensitive radio traffic is scrambled and encrypted, and therefore beyond the means of an operative to make sense of. However, transmissions are sometimes made 'in clear' either due to sloppy procedures or between less security-conscious operators. There is little chance of an operative making much sense of traffic between the Soviet Northern Fleet and its base, but guerrillas in Angola might not have encrypted radio equipment available.

 COMINT and ELINT are often very useful against mundane targets, but some of the entities of Our Other Enemy emit fields that scramble or degrade the quality of electronic devices. -N

 I have seen taps blown out, bugs fired, and once an operative bleed from the ears while listening to a tape. Though the last one may have just been a Dylan album. – Miller

If COMINT is to be any use, operatives must understand the language in which transmissions are made and any codes used. These are rarely complex in third-world militaries; call signs are often egotistical rather than deceptive, and even in the armies of major powers there can be a tendency to match a call sign to a unit type. Thus it is sometimes possible to discern from a call sign alone whether a unit is 'teeth' or 'tail', and whether it is armoured, infantry or artillery based. Thermal (infrared) cameras can be used for surveillance under some circumstances, though the image can be difficult to make out by an untrained observer. One of the most important uses of thermal technology is detection rather than surveillance; the thermal device will indicate that a person is present even if it is not possible to tell what they are doing. Other means can then be used to observe the subject.

Likewise, thermal cameras will indicate if a vehicle's engine is running or has been running recently; the same goes for generators and other equipment. Knowing that a remote building has power may be useful even if it is not possible to see what is going on inside.

Low-light (sometimes called 'starlight') vision devices are also available, though they tend to be quite bulky and/or fragile. Work is underway to develop a military-grade starlight scope that can be fitted to a weapon, and this will probably become available in the next few years. For now, however, various experimental and special-purpose low-light systems are available. These do not make vision possible in total blackness, but they can enable a subject to be observed in near-darkness. Care should be taken not to look at light sources as the device's technology amplifies light.

LISTENING DEVICES

The most common technical means used by surveillance and intelligence personnel are listening devices of various sorts.

The simplest of these, in terms of technical sophistication and ease of use, are telephone taps. Most telephones are unsecured, making it possible to listen in on a conversation by 'tapping' into the line at an exchange or junction box.

However, the presence of a tap sometimes causes a slight sound on the line that can give away its presence. Since taps can be readily used against us, operatives should be alert for such signals. A simple rule is never to say anything on the telephone that you would not want to be overheard by hostile intelligence personnel.

One way to avoid a tap is to use a different line. This may sound obvious but a person under surveillance might use a public phone or one connected to a different exchange for private conversations. Of course, the recipient has to do the same if the tap is between the receiving phone and their local exchange; an operative should not make the error of assuming that just because they used a public phone in a different part of the city their calls are secure.

Secure phone lines, which use scrambler systems, are available but are not 100% proof against penetration by intelligence operatives. The equipment needed to descramble a conversation is not portable and as a result will be unavailable to operatives in foreign countries. However, embassies and similar installations will have 'secure' phone lines with this sort of technology, and it may be available if circumstances merit the effort required to deploy it.

Internal telephone communication tends to be unsecured, and conversations are often unguarded. It may be possible to plant a tap or a recording device on an internal phone line such as one between two parts of a base. Lines that run under a river between military or political facilities are often unsecured, due to the difficulty of getting at them to plant a tap. If operatives can get access somehow, a wealth of information might be extracted.

 Learn to be creative when using telephone taps. Often the employment of these devices requires that a superior sign off on them. While

some high-ranking officers will leave the details and discretion to the operative, many more want to make sure their own careers are safe. With scandal being such a common cause of early career termination, it does push some into an overly conservative viewpoint.   -N

Conversations within a building can be monitored with a variety of listening devices, or 'bugs'. These are usually planted somewhere that gives good concealment but which does not impede their ability to overhear a conversation. Air ducts and the like are good locations, but not if there are noisy fans nearby.

Some bugs record conversations and must be retrieved to collect their data, which can be hazardous. Others transmit using radio and picked up by nearby receivers. The range of any bug is short, making it necessary for operatives to place themselves and their receiver close to the target. Good security procedures may make this impossible. Often the buildings close to a sensitive location are occupied by people performing innocuous tasks from whom no useful information can be obtained; controlling these buildings makes it very difficult for operatives to get close enough to receive signals from bugs. This is only possible for large-scale operations, however, and is more likely to be done by a network operating on friendly turf. A network operating in a foreign city will not have the luxury of creating such a buffer zone against bugs.

Bugs can be detected in a variety of ways. A physical search of likely locations is the most obvious, but those that transmit can also be detected by using a receiver that sweeps across many frequencies. This will only detect a bug that is transmitting; some devices do not constantly transmit and may be missed by a sweep.

Bugs must be planted or otherwise brought into a secure area to be useful. Their power supply does not last forever, and in some cases they have to be retrieved to obtain their information. The best defence against bugs is the physical security of a location. Places that are hard to get into such as well-secured ducts are also hard to plant a bug in, and potential suspects who might plant one – such as someone disguised as a cleaner – should not be left unobserved for long enough to both plant a bug and return the area to its previous condition. Damage to fittings, signs of furniture or shelving being moved and similar disturbances may indicate that a bug has been planted or retrieved.

An alternative to bugging is to get as close as possible to the subject in a neighbouring room or building and place microphones or simply listen. It may be possible to break through a wall in a neighbouring building and create a listening space within an embassy or other supposedly secure location. Power sockets and similar utilities often have a space behind them which can be accessed without going through the secured part of the building. Care must be taken to avoid making noise that will be heard in the target area – sound travels both ways!

It is also possible to hear what is happening inside a building by using a laser or infrared beam targeted on a window. Sounds inside the building will cause very small vibrations in the glass, which can be picked up by sensitive equipment as it reflects the beam. Equipment of this sort is rather bulky and hard to conceal, so is typically used from within a facing building. Operatives concerned about their own security may consider holding sensitive conversations in a room with no windows. Of course, the enemy can do the same.

BUGS AND OTHER REMOTE LISTENING DEVICES

See *World War Cthulhu: Cold War* pg. 161 for more details of the varieties and uses of listening devices, and methods for detecting them.

ON-SITE ANALYSIS

In the normal course of operations, raw data is fed back 'up the chain' to analysts at home. Their task is to sift and collate it and to draw conclusion, just as the operative's is to ensure that the data collected is as complete and accurate as possible. It is not normally desirable for an operative to attempt analysis; their well-intended efforts can confuse an issue or render a piece of critical information invalid or obscure.

However, there are times when operatives in the field or at the network's headquarters must engage in some analysis of data in order to plan a mission or to decide what to do next. At its most basic, this analysis includes deciding where to place surveillance posts to observe a given subject, which might require analysis of the subject's lifestyle and habits.

In a wider sense, much can be learned from simple observations filtered through a keen mind. Any field analysis will be of the quick-and-dirty sort, and can lead to erroneous conclusions if the operative has limited data to

work from. However, local observations can be highly useful in drawing short-term conclusions valid for the immediate area of operations.

You will be the on-site analyst for most missions. Sending information up the chain of command is too great of a security risk for our organisation. Do not trouble yourself: you would not be in this position if you could not handle it, nor will you be for long. -N

By way of example, an untrained observer might be quite capable of noting that there are soldiers guarding an installation, but a skilled operative can learn much more from their equipment, insignia and methods. Troops that are sloppy in dress and who leave equipment lying around are unlikely to be of high calibre. The same can be said for those who run predictable, unimaginative patrol routines or highly erratic, half-hearted ones.

High-quality formations tend to be equipped with more modern vehicles and weaponry, including anti-aircraft and anti-tank systems, or at the very least will have equipment that is well maintained and properly secured. Likewise, high-end formations tend to undertake drills and training even when deployed to guard an area; poor-quality units will goof off and go to seed in such a role.

Do you know the common ranks, branches of service and units of your opposition? Of course you do. You can tell Soviet Army troops from Border Troops at a glance. But what about the various types of Our Other Enemy? True, this knowledge is dangerous on a practically cellular level, but it is necessary. – Rodriquez

Simple extrapolation from these clues will tell an operative what the enemy is likely to do in the event of an alert. Poor units might not notice thefts or an infiltration to steal documents, and in many cases fear of the 'vertical stroke' (the wrath of high command descending through everyone in the chain of command down to the person who actually screwed up) will cause such units to conceal problems rather than report them. The enemy might actually conspire to conceal our operatives' actions!

Poor-quality units will also respond sluggishly to an alert, and in an inept manner. Personnel are far more likely to fall for a diversion or deception, and again might assist us by making mistakes that confuse the situation. If an enemy patrol can be induced to start shooting at shadows in one area, a covert operations team will have a much easier time getting in and out of the objective.

Conversely, a high-end formation will react quickly and effectively. It will put out aggressive and imaginative patrols that do far more than amble along a well-defined path, occasionally looking around. Knowing that the force securing an objective is such a formation tells us a lot about the target's importance, but also about the risks inherent in trying to infiltrate it.

One very important consideration is whether the forces guarding an area are police (or perhaps paramilitary security units), regular soldiers or a political formation such as the Soviet NKVD. Again, this tells us a lot about the objective as well as how the force guarding it will act when alerted.

Political troops in Warsaw pact countries have far more latitude about using violence than ordinary soldiers or police. NKVD and similar political troops are more likely to open fire than those with less political clout, due to greater confidence that they will avoid any consequences for their actions.

On-site analysis of the quick-and-dirty sort may also be necessary when deciding how urgent a piece of information is. Much of the data gathered by surveillance is routine, and whilst useful it is not worth making a special effort to report it. Other information is low-priority; the appearance of a new type of military truck is something that the intelligence services need to know about sooner or later but it is hard to imagine a situation where reporting it is of great urgency.

All information is useful and should be reported when possible, but at times the operative in the field needs to make a decision about what needs to be reported immediately and what can wait for a safer opportunity.

You know the books we sometimes get our hands on? Don't look in them. Ever.
– Miller

REPORTING BACK

As already noted, it is not desirable for operatives to carry out their own analysis; we have experts for that. Even if a quick-and-dirty analysis is carried out in the field, what goes back 'up the chain' must be the raw data. Our analysts will decide what is relevant and what is not; they will put two and two together from first principles. This requires that they are working from first principles and that data has not been unintentionally altered by attempts to collate and analyse it further down the chain.

Reports can vary considerably in length and content. Ideally, all data must be passed back but often this is not possible. Moving vast volumes of record cards or paper can be a problem at the best of times; doing it whilst crossing a hostile border is well-nigh impossible. Thus a report must be tailored to the means used to transmit it and to the circumstances surrounding it. Wherever possible, however, our analysts should be presented with as much raw data as we can transmit to them.

You are probably used to having to gather a large amount of data to present to your superiors, especially if there is a need to build a criminal case or gain enough proof so that a diplomat can be sent home. This is not the case with Our Other Enemy. You just need enough intel to know when, who, what and where. The rest is up to you. I kind of like that simplicity.
– Rodriquez

ANALYSING INFORMATION

If the investigators need to make a quick on-site analysis of the material they have gathered, this will usually be covered by either Military Science or Tradecraft rolls, depending on the type of intelligence. At the Keeper's discretion, an appropriate weapons or vehicle skill may be used for background knowledge about military equipment instead.

Of course, members of Section 46 may also need to use the Cthulhu Mythos skill for on-site analysis as part of their true missions. It is rarely advisable to carry Mythos tomes around in the field, and communications may not be possible over normal channels, so there is sometimes no substitute for a head full of dangerous and blasphemous knowledge.

This follows a well-established principle that information is like a wedge. Operatives at the sharp end should have only the information that they need to carry out their missions, whilst analysts should have every single scrap of data that can be gathered. If the means to transmit a piece of information without compromising the security of the network exists then it should be reported.

Operatives should not be concerned with what seems relevant, and should also not make judgements about what might be misleading or deliberately deceptive. It is the business of analysts to find deceptions or concealed truths, and for this they need all the information they can get. Also, there is the danger that an operative 'on the ground' might discard a piece of information because they think it is untrue when in fact the 'big picture' would reveal that it is not.

Similarly, no piece of information is trivial. Data that is already known may provide corroboration of information obtained by other methods, and can serve as a guide to the reliability of new information. Indeed, the absence of certain data can tell analysts a lot, particularly when the enemy is trying to deceive us. However, the analysts need to be sure that this information was genuinely not present rather than being omitted from a report for other reasons.

No piece of information is of any use until it has been reported, analysed and passed to the planners for use. This all takes time, which can be in short supply. Some information must be transmitted immediately to have any value, and some is so important that it must be passed back up the chain as quickly as possible. Most routine information, however, is not so time-dependent. Operatives in the field must balance the importance making a full and timely report against the security risks. Few data items are worth a 'blown' network or even a single asset.

 When do you report back? Only in the direst of circumstances should you break security and contact us during a mission. Generally, you will know how to do so before you depart, and are trusted to maintain the strictest security at all times. If you are not given any means of reporting back until the mission is completed, you are neither expected nor desired to do so. -N

Keep your lies straight, especially the big ones. Lying about those things that live in the cracks is hard, mate. You never know who's seen them, or who they've seen.
Am I me or a cover, cover?
What is inside, inside the pages of me.
I need a break, a holiday, holiday. Good thing the Guvnor, the Guvnor is sending a couple of blokes to give me a lift. I should get my rest then, then.
Oh god do I need a kip. - Stanton

CHAPTER FIVE

PERSONAL VIOLENCE

· PERSONAL VIOLENCE ·

Most of the violence done by our operatives is on a personal scale. A single guard may have to be eliminated or a key member of an enemy organisation might be targeted for assassination. Violence of this sort falls into two main categories: targeted and facilitation. Targeted violence usually means assassination of a key figure, and may be the primary or a secondary objective of a mission. It must be planned for not only in terms of how and when the act will be carried out, but also in terms of what the effects will be and what response is likely to be made by the enemy.

Sometimes it will not be appropriate to simply assassinate the target. It may be necessary to make the killing look accidental or like a crime rather than an intelligence operation. It may be desirable that the target simply disappears and is never found – if this can be combined with planted evidence that they were eliminated by their own side, have defected to the enemy or have vanished in some other potentially damaging circumstance, then additional benefits may accrue from the elimination.

Either way, care must be taken to ensure that the target is eliminated correctly, which may require that a carefully planned and halfway-executed operation be aborted at the point of success.

 You don't need to kill everyone in a cell of cattle in order to eliminate it. If you are certain that most are dabblers in the works of Our Other Enemy, or are unlikely to recover from a loss of leadership, then take out the leaders. One won't be enough; take out the entire inner circle to be sure. – Rodriquez

 Rodriquez is a little too soft on this one. Eliminate them all and you won't have to worry about the cell springing up again. – Miller

Facilitation violence is directed at anyone who is in the way at the time. Guards, drivers, people wearing a uniform the operative needs and similar targets may need to be eliminated in order for the mission to proceed, to evade detection or to obtain a necessary item. Facilitation violence may or may not be planned.

Eliminating a courier to get a case or an official to obtain a security pass may be an essential part of an operation;

as such this should be planned as carefully as the primary mission. The act must be covert and timely; the elimination must be performed such that the enemy does not have time to realise something is amiss, and must be sufficiently discreet as to go unnoticed at least until the mission is complete.

Some facilitation violence is of an impromptu nature. An unexpected guard or other hostile who is in the way may need to be removed. It is not possible to plan for such eventualities other than in the most general of terms, such as by practising stealth and deception along with silent killing techniques. However, where possible guards should be evaded or otherwise bypassed rather than killed. Even if the elimination is silent, the body may be found or the victim missed. From the first killing in an operation the clock begins to run down. Hiding bodies can slow down the process, but not indefinitely.

Some targets are best left alone no matter what. Local police will usually search vigorously for the killer of one of their own even if they would not make much effort if the victim was a civilian or a rich man's bodyguard. Public officials and high-prominence citizens will also cause a stir if they are killed.

There are times when even if we are willing to take such an overt action in the knowledge that the enemy's intelligence apparatus will be set against us, we will still choose not to stir up the region's law enforcement as well. The two are often not connected even in countries where they are on the same side. On neutral ground the enemy's intelligence apparatus will be unlikely to cooperate with the local police.

Thus it may be necessary to abort an operation if it will bring a response that is more widespread than we are ready for. We are effectively at war with the enemy's intelligence services, but not necessarily their police or the enforcers of the local crime cartel. Long-term goals will be compromised by making an entire region hostile to us; trying to conduct intelligence operations in the midst of a manhunt is tricky at best.

It is necessary to build into an operational plan just how much facilitation violence is acceptable and what targets absolutely must not be attacked. An abort is frustrating but the alternative will be much worse. Violence is a tool, but one that must be used with precision.

TAKING DIRECT ACTION

Direct action is rare in intelligence work, and under normal circumstances it is only used after a careful period of planning and set-up. Action should be short and decisive; the longer an operative is engaged, the greater the chance that something will go badly wrong. For example, snatching a foreign diplomatic courier or a suspected spy should take no more than a few seconds and give the target no chance to resist. A bungled snatch that results in a fight or a pursuit might attract local law enforcement or other intervention whether it ultimately succeeds or not.

Thus a good set-up is vital, followed by swift and decisive action taken without hesitation. Poor setup can result in the operation failing from the outset, whereas bad execution can sometimes be dealt with by improvisation and determination. Poor execution can, however, result in complications – a simple document snatch could end up with the operative trying to evade a pursuit by a whole city's police force as well as hostile intelligence operatives.

Our Other Enemy can take many forms, and that simple cattle might actually be the master. There are tainted lineages that can pass as human, things that can consume a person's insides and wear them as a mask, and other things that puppet people. Make sure of your target before you strike. – Rodriquez

Sometimes, there is no alternative but to use violence in either a planned or unplanned manner. The former is much safer, as good planning permits many variables to be controlled and the dice to be loaded before the order to commence is given. However, in the situation where something has gone awry or an operative must evade capture, it may be necessary for the operative to think on their feet and use violence wherever necessary. Violent action should be taken suddenly, ideally by surprise, and with overwhelming force at the key point.

More than this, though, action must be taken with an aim in mind. Intelligence operatives do not skirmish with the enemy for the sake of it; every shot fired or blow struck must be in accordance with a deliberate aim. That may be the completion of a mission or the removal of an obstacle, but it must take the operative closer to his aim. If the object is to escape capture then winning a gunfight is irrelevant unless it is furthers that aim. An opportunity to escape is worth more than eliminating a couple more pursuers. Operatives who forget this rule can become engrossed in the fight rather than working towards their chosen outcome.

The servants of Our Other Enemy frequently must be eliminated in a permanent and satisfying manner. Use the same procedure you would for any other such act. You might even find it liberating to not need as much red tape to effect a clear and decisive goal. –N

PERSONAL COMBAT

Where it is necessary to engage in combat, either armed or otherwise, the most important factor is precise and deliberate action. This must be ferocious and violent, but

always controlled. If it is necessary to fight at all then it is necessary to do whatever it takes to win.

A wounded enemy might shoot an operative in the back, or could give information that will lead enemy intelligence services to the operative. Hesitation to shoot or strike may give bodyguards an opportunity to act or the target a chance to escape. Be ruthless but not vindictive; operatives are willing to kill if the situation merits it but do not seek to do so for any reason other than the mission.

Stealth, deception and positioning can be used to give the operative the advantage if they have initiated the combat; they must be willing to withdraw if the odds are not good. Remember that a failed attack on a target will result in a state of alert and an active search for the attackers. If the option is available the operative should weigh the chances of success now against the possibility of a better opportunity later.

Sometimes the operative will not have a choice whether or not to engage in combat, such as when they are fired upon by hostiles after being detected in the course of a mission. In this case the odds will likely be poor; an operative is almost certain to be outnumbered, at least after a short time as additional hostiles arrive, and may be outgunned. The goal in this case is survival and escape; firing a weapon is likely a poor option. Concentrating on driving or evading the enemy is a better alternative, especially in the dark where a muzzle flash will give their location away. Holding fire and slipping away is likely to be a better option.

Similar comments apply to personal combat with hand weapons or when unarmed. If the operative has the choice of whether or not to enter combat then they can strike suddenly and unexpectedly. This is the key to success when eliminating a sentry or snatching a target. If, on the other hand, the operative is attacked, by hostiles trying to detain him for example, then the goal is to instead facilitate escape rather than defeat his opponents.

If an opponent can be downed or pushed into a place they cannot quickly get out of, the operative has a chance to escape. There may be little point in finishing off a guard if others are on the way, although if the only person who has seen which way the operative is headed can be killed or rendered unconscious then this may be worthwhile as it facilitates escape.

 Even the most mundane-looking of the servants of Our Other Enemy may possess personal abilities beyond the norm. It might seem like a well-placed bullet should suffice, but there have been instances where this has not been the case. Researching your target and getting a firm concept of its abilities is even more crucial than with a mundane direct action mission. -N

In general, body blows that wind the target or kicks to their knees can be useful in slowing pursuit and facilitating escape, and may be a better option than trying for a knock-out punch. An operative who strikes bone with a closed fist risks damaging their hand, which can subsequently make it impossible to operate a weapon. Open-hand strikes are a far better option.

An operative should only have to engage in unarmed combat when caught completely by surprise or when attempting to abduct a target. At any other time they should be able to procure a weapon of some kind. This may be purpose-built, such as a fighting knife, but could be any improvised weapon.

USING IMPROVISED WEAPONS

In *Call of Cthulhu*, use of improvised weapons generally falls under the Fighting (Brawl) or Throw skills, depending on whether or not they are used hand-to-hand. Some items are less suitable for weapons, as they are unwieldy, poorly balanced or painful to hold (such as a hot poker); in such cases, the Keeper may assign a penalty die to anyone using them.

When it comes to determining the damage inflicted by improvised weapons, the table on pg. 401 of the *Call of Cthulhu* rulebook has many examples that may be used as inspiration. In general, small items will inflict 1D4 of damage, medium ones 1D6, and large or heavy items 1D8. Sharp or pointed items may also impale.

Virtually any object can be used as a weapon. Kitchen knives are an obvious choice but screwdrivers and most other stiff and narrow objects can deliver a puncture wound. Blunt implements such as hammers, bricks, typewriters and even soup cans can all be used as weapons.

An operative who is caught unarmed can usually find a weapon of some kind within seconds, if they apply a little ingenuity. Unarmed combat skills can be used to acquire a suitable weapon from a target with which to finish the job. Failing all else, basic grappling skills can be used to cause the opponent to fall, after which a quick stomp will put them out of action.

Use of Firearms

Most of the time, an operative will be armed only with a handgun – if they are armed at all. A handgun has the advantages of being light and concealable, and can be quickly brought to bear; but they do not penetrate cover well and have a short accurate range. More importantly, even with a two-handed shooting stance most people – even highly trained people – cannot hit a distant target reliably with a handgun.

Handguns are valuable mainly because they can be carried where larger weapons cannot. They are not a good choice for sustained combat or for fighting at even moderate range, but are entirely capable of inflicting fatal injuries. A handgun is well suited to close range assassination and any gunshot will tend to slow pursuit. When a team is clearing an area a handgun is a good choice of weapon for an operative expected to be operating controls or opening doors.

Quick and accurate handgun shooting is arguably the most important combat skill learned by an operative as it is likely to be the most readily available weapon. Operatives should learn to operate a range of weapons; slight differences in positioning of safety catches, magazine release and the like can be critical when an enemy's weapon is taken in the middle of a desperate encounter.

If serious combat seems likely, the operative should first consider whether it is better to avoid it altogether. If not, then a larger weapon is probably required. Submachine guns are a reasonable compromise between handling and firepower. They tend to be short and light enough to be quickly brought to bear, and are well suited to operations in buildings or vehicles.

Very small submachine guns are actually less accurate than handguns as the recoil of their automatic fire disrupts careful aiming. Larger and longer submachine guns are more precise but also require more room to use. Very small submachine guns (or machine pistols as they are sometimes called) such as the Vz61 Skorpion are best suited to close-range assassination rather than sustained combat, whereas larger weapons are useful in combat out to fairly long ranges.

Submachine guns are a favourite weapon of bodyguards and security forces. They are intimidating when displayed and give the user the capability to lay down withering firepower to cover extraction of the principal they are protecting or to quickly down a threat. Submachine guns and shotguns are the most likely 'bigger guns' encountered by an operative in the course of a mission.

Many entities will shrug off fire from handguns, and you may be tempted to use heavier weapons. Those that can ignore a pistol can usually be trusted to ignore a rifle as well. Paradoxically, there are credible reports of entities that can shake off a bullet but are vulnerable to a blade. The downside, of course, is that if you are close enough to stab it, it likely has a host of nasty appendages to tear you apart with. -N

Yeah, cemetery creepers are said to be immune to bullets, but a large enough volume of fire will put one down. The problem is, there is usually more than one. Adding to this, the close confines of their habitats makes volumes of fire tricky to produce. – Rodriguez

A shotgun offers many of the advantages of a submachine gun, and will often have superior knock-down power. Whereas a submachine gun delivers a stream of bullets, some of which might miss, a shotgun at close range delivers all its pellets to the target at once. The result can instantly disable an opponent and can also be used to destroy door locks and hinges. However, shotguns poorly penetrate cover and body armour, and are effective only at quite short range as their pellets quickly lose their velocity. The large bore of a shotgun is an excellent deterrent to violence or incentive to cooperation.

Rifles offer very good penetration and accuracy at range, especially full-bore or 'battle rifle' calibre weapons such as the 7.62x51mm FN FAL used by the British army. However, such weapons are not easily concealed and are most likely to be employed for sniping or overwatch as operatives carry out a mission. Assault rifles are shorter and lighter, and usually capable of fully automatic fire. This will quickly disable most targets at short range and can be used to suppress enemies at greater distances by putting a lot of rounds close to their position.

Firing a weapon 'from the hip' or one-handed whilst moving is extremely inaccurate and virtually guarantees the firer will miss. However, it may be that all is required is to force the enemy to take cover whilst the operative retreats or continues the mission. Operatives should be mindful of the value of suppressive fire, and should be willing to expend ammunition to keep enemies under cover when appropriate. It is not always necessary to 'win' a gunfight; what matters is completing the mission or evading capture.

FIRING FROM THE HIP

Firing from the hip incurs a penalty die to attack rolls, but the attacker will be able to travel their MOV rate x5 yards in a combat round. This may also allow the attacker to lay down suppressing fire (see pg. 126 of the *Call of Cthulhu* rulebook).

STEALTH AND CONCEALMENT

It is a well-proven concept that when attempting to avoid detection, an operative should only move when necessary. Movement makes noise and attracts the eye; more so when that movement is rapid. The basic concept is 'low and slow', making use of shadows and all available cover.

It is possible for an operative to move through fairly open terrain without being detected if they possess some form of camouflage; the less cover there is, the slower the operative must move. Few people have the patience to do this under the stress of field conditions, however; most personnel will lose their nerve upon feeling exposed for too long and will dash into cover. Similarly, the only way to avoid detection when a dark scene is suddenly illuminated is to freeze in place; movement will certainly be spotted, but whilst remaining still is something of a gamble, it is the best of a bad set of options.

In rural terrain, military camouflage is useful for concealed movement. Disruptive pattern clothing breaks up the shape of the human body, though the head and face tend to attract the eye. A shapeless soft hat and face veil of a sort used by snipers will work well, and applying colouration to the face to make it less obvious is also effective. If camouflage paints

are not available, mud will work. However, if the operative is spotted whilst camouflaged then there is no chance to provide a cover story. Camouflage will be recognised as such, ensuring that the enemy knows that the operative is up to no good. Less effective camouflage such as dark-coloured civilian clothing is still useful for concealment and may be explained away. Dark colours such as blue and green are best; black is 'too dark' and tends to stand out from the surroundings.

In the urban terrain where most operations take place, rural camouflage is generally inappropriate. If stealth is required, then a combination of dark clothing, use of cover and shadows, and waiting for observers to be distracted must suffice. In general, if there are other people about and there is some plausible reason for being in the area it is better to use misdirection or deception than stealth; openly walking around as if the operative has every right to be there might avoid detection far better than skulking through the bushes.

For operations where there is no plausible cover story, such as entering the guarded compound of a prominent local figure, there may be no alternative to stealth followed by a 'loud' phase. Loud in this case typically means shooting with unsuppressed firearms; in other words, the complete abandonment of any pretence at stealth. Somewhere between the stealthy and loud phases is a situation where the operative takes actions that will eventually be discovered and which cannot be taken as anything but hostile.

By way of example, shooting a guard with an unsuppressed handgun is 'loud'; eliminating him silently with a knife is not, but it still changes the situation. The dead guard will eventually be found (or at least noted as missing from his post) and an alert will be sounded. It is not absolutely certain that a mission will go loud from this point on, but it is likely. Speed becomes more important than stealth at this juncture, though it is usually possible to evade detection long enough to break contact with guards or other hostiles. For this reason operatives should not switch to a 'loud mindset' but must be able to judge whether stealth or speed and aggression are the best options at that particular moment – and to act accordingly.

In a situation where there is no plausible cover story and the operative has to rely on stealth, it may seem that the best option is to go in armed for battle. However, this is not always the case. Guards who are not expecting an attack may hesitate, or might choose to investigate rather than shooting or sounding an alarm, if they are unsure of what is happening. Someone blatantly marching across the countryside with a rifle presents a fairly clear situation,

whereas what appears to be a lost tourist may provoke a different response – at least long enough for the operative to deal with the situation.

There is always the possibility of people uninvolved with the mission being alarmed at seeing armed personnel and informing the local police. If at all possible the operative should dress and act in a manner that creates ambiguity about their intention and identity. A guard who would open fire on an armed intruder might instead confront a group of drunks wandering home and send them on their way with a blow or two. This creates an opportunity to deal with the situation without going loud.

Unless a team of operatives has a reason to move and act like a military force (for example, when armed and in a restricted area) they should conceal their weapons and behave like ordinary people. Movement that is too purposeful can attract attention; too little chatter is surprisingly obvious. A group that acts like it has a completely innocent reason for being where it is might elicit a 'chase off' response rather than a hostile one – there are usually repercussions when guards open fire and most are quite reluctant to do so.

USE OF EXPLOSIVES AND INCENDIARY DEVICES

Explosives come in two basic types: low explosives and high explosives. Low explosives (for example gunpowder) explode relatively slowly and create a pushing effect that is useful for moving rubble or demolishing light structures. High explosives (such as TNT or various military explosives)

explode more quickly and have a cutting effect. Low explosives push things around; high explosives pulverise them.

Both types have their use on a mission, and operatives may additionally find incendiary devices highly effective too. Incendiaries cause fires or destroy materials by burning. An explosion might cause a fire, but there is no guarantee. Placing an incendiary device in a flammable building or near materials will almost certainly cause it to catch fire and burn fiercely.

 Fire is said to cleanse, but experience has taught us that not all entities are susceptible to such ministrations. Fire does attract attention, usually of the official kind, but the use of fire can bring a horde of civilians running to the source. This makes too many witnesses to easily disperse, much less distract, misdirect or eliminate. -N

Explosives have many applications, none of which are particularly subtle. Where possible, operatives should use pre-packed explosives of known quantity so that the effects of an explosion can be predicted. Home-made or improvised explosives are less reliable in terms of detonation and effect, but can be useful if carefully used.

Explosives and incendiary devices can be used for anti-personnel or anti-materiel work, and for many such applications a military grenade is an ideal package. There are two common incendiary grenade types. White phosphorous grenades burn on contact with air and throw fragments of burning phosphorous out to several feet away. These will set most materials they touch alight and pose a severe threat to nearby personnel. White phosphorous also produces a dense cloud of smoke, but it is not a 'smoke grenade' as such.

Thermite grenades are heavy but burn very hot; hot enough to destroy an artillery piece if the grenade is placed in the breech or dropped down the barrel. Thermite will set almost anything alight and will even melt steel. Its anti-personnel use is limited as it cannot be thrown far and does not project burning material. However, thermite is an excellent means of destroying even solid metal objects.

Many hand grenades are of a fragmentation type, which have a small blast radius but fling pieces of sharp metal (comprising the casing, plus notched wire wrapped around the bursting charge) out to a considerable distance. This is extremely dangerous to nearby personnel but has limited blast effects; it may initiate other explosives but will probably not do critical damage to structures.

Most high explosives require a fairly high initiation energy. Heat is unlikely to be enough to set off an explosive, and expedients such as shooting dynamite will not initiate it if it is in good condition. A small explosion is the usual means of initiation, typically provided by a blasting cap, which is in turn set off by a timer or electrical impulse.

Primers of this sort are usually produced from less-powerful explosives that require less energy to detonate them. A grenade or similar explosive device will also suffice, but this has limitations in terms of how and when the detonation occurs. Some high explosives, such as nitroglycerine, are unstable and may detonate if struck hard.

Low explosives such as gunpowder can usually be set off by heat. A burning fuse may be enough to set off a powder charge, which will then initiate more stable explosives located next to it. Low explosives are also far easier to improvise than more powerful ones.

Explosives and incendiary devices must be tailored to the intended application. For anti-personnel work, any explosive will create blast and heat which will endanger people nearby. However, the behaviour of blast in built-up areas is complex; blast is a shock wave of air pushed away from the explosion and can be redirected or reflected by hard surfaces, causing areas of increased destruction and other places that are almost untouched.

To ensure maximum anti-personnel effect, explosives can be packed with loose material that will be flung out when the explosion occurs. This could take the form of a nail bomb (an explosive device surrounded by nails or other small heavy objects that will act as projectiles) or might be improvised from local materials.

STATS FOR VARIOUS EXPLOSIVES

See the Appendices for more about explosive devices and grenades.

Destruction of objects such as a vehicle or piece of machinery can be accomplished in many ways. A sizeable internal explosion or incendiary device will cause at least some damage to most objects and vehicles; a thermite grenade placed on the engine deck of a tank will burn right through the engine and wreck the vehicle. Similar mayhem will be caused to any other machinery attacked in this manner. Ideally, a high explosive 'cutting' charge should be placed at a critical point to cripple or destroy machinery; low explosives might simply cause distortion and minor damage to heavy machinery.

For the demolition of structures, it is necessary to place charges quite precisely. Steel and concrete supports can be cut with high explosives using a fairly small charge provided it is correctly placed. Low explosives may merely push some parts of the structure, around which may not be enough to collapse it; though a weakened bridge or other structure might still be denied to the enemy until major repairs are undertaken.

Even if use of explosives is peripheral to a mission, such as blowing something up to cause a diversion, then it is still critical that the demolition succeeds. If a gate must be blasted open to allow access or exfiltration then failure will compromise the mission. The only time demolition can be considered non-critical is when operatives engage in additional sabotage or destruction on an opportunistic basis. This is useful under some circumstances but should not be permitted to interfere with the primary mission.

It is important that explosives are handled by an operative trained in their use. Mines, grenades and the like can be employed by anyone who knows how to emplace them, but setting a charge requires calculations that are beyond the capabilities of untrained operatives. Only in the most desperate circumstances should an untrained operative take a best guess and go for it. In such situations it is important to err on the side of massive overkill; failed demolition at three points is worth a lot less than one extravagant piece of destruction.

The only good kill is overkill, make sure you did the job right and you won't have to do it again. - Miller

HANDLING DEMOLITION TASKS

Not all intelligence personnel are trained in the use of explosives, but many quick-and-dirty demolitions do not require much skill. Anyone can drop a thermite grenade into a tank or stick a limpet mine on the side of a ship. The question in this case is not usually one of success or failure, but degree of success; a badly placed limpet mine might not sink a ship, but it will certainly cause some damage provided it does not fall off. Most intelligence personnel are smart enough to be shown how to ensure this does not happen.

Complex demolitions such as bringing down a bridge or derailing a train in motion require the attentions of a skilled operative and can take some time. Calculating stress points and charge sizes is not the stuff of exciting adventures, so a demolition of this sort is best used as a matter of plot. The time required to set up the explosives is a 'clock'; the site must be kept clear of interference for this time. Just getting to the demolition site can also be an adventure, requiring removal of obstacles, elimination of guards and the like.

Skill rolls may still be required to ensure the demolition goes as planned, but for the most part the actual demolition work can be fairly routine. Facilitating it is the stuff of adventure.

SILENT KILLING

The key to any sort of silent killing is surprise. An opponent who cries out or kicks things over will likely attract attention, and an enemy who discharges a weapon will certainly do so. Efficiency is vital; the longer a kill takes the more likely noise becomes. Generally a close approach is required, using stealth or deception. Infiltration might be assisted by sniper cover using a suppressed weapon, but this still makes a fair amount of noise and is only useful in a situation where there is already a fair amount of sound to cover the shots.

A silent killing technique must cause the target to die, or be rendered incapable of speech and action, in a short time. For this reason firearms, even extremely quiet ones, are chancy. At very close range a headshot or a round into the heart will cause near-instantaneous disablement, but even a slight variation in the aim point can permit the target to raise the alarm or even begin fighting back.

Techniques that would be useful for an assassination, such as shooting repeatedly into the abdomen, kidneys or liver to cause fatal blood loss, or the lungs to prevent breathing, may take too long to be effective as silent kills.

Firearms must be used very precisely if at all. It is tempting to consider a gun as the easy method compared with sneaking close enough to use a knife, but to be certain of a silent kill a gunman must be close enough that a knife becomes a viable option. It must also be reiterated that there is no such thing as a completely silent firearm. Even the very best make at least a little noise; most suppressed guns simply make less noise than an unsuppressed one, not no noise.

Some fairly crude methods are entirely workable. A heavy blow to the back of the skull with a blunt instrument will usually cause immediate unconsciousness, and even if it does not it should render the target vulnerable to a finishing move. A blow heavy enough to crack the skull will often cause death, though not necessarily instantly.

Thus, clubbing an opponent over the head is a reasonably effective method of facilitating a quick kill or disablement, though it does impose the risk of the target falling hard and causing secondary noise. A blow from behind is best; even someone caught by surprise may be able to defend against one from within his field of vision, and it is rather hard to disguise this action.

Sharp, pointed implements are far more effective. A blow almost anywhere other than the head is survivable and will usually produce a lot of noise from the target. Death can be caused most quickly by cutting the major arteries; specifically the inside of the thigh, the inside of the upper arm, the neck and the torso behind the collar bone. The latter requires a downward stabbing motion which was perfected by wartime commando trainers and used effectively in many theatres. A stab from behind into the kidney area can also cause rapid disablement and death.

It wasn't human. I found that out when I slipped the garrotte around its neck and pulled it in tight. No carotids, maybe. So I kept hold and used my knife on its kidney. No kidneys of course. After that, things got a bit hectic... – Miller

The key in all these cases is to keep the target quiet; in terms of vocal noise, dropped items and knocking objects over – until they are dead or unconscious. This can take many seconds, so the usual method is to grab the target from behind, placing a hand over the mouth before delivering the fatal knife stroke. It is possible to cut the vocal chords, usually by a thrust into the neck from the side and then pulling the knife to cut. However, this takes precision and will be accompanied by a great deal of blood loss. It is impossible to avoid being stained by blood when attempting this manoeuvre.

SPOT RULES FOR SILENT KILLS

Mechanically, silent kills can be treated as a special application of the *Striking the First Blow (Surprise)* rules found on pg. 106 of the *Call of Cthulhu* rulebook. The main difference is the requirement that the strike be silent; this may be handled by using a combined Fighting (Brawl) and Stealth roll for the attack.

Strangulation, whether with a garrotte, clothing or by manual means, is an effective and surprisingly quick method of killing. Closing off the windpipe makes it difficult for the target to breathe or call out but can take an extended time to render them unconscious. Instead, what is necessary is to compress the carotid arteries that supply oxygenated blood to the brain. These are at the sides of the neck and are best compressed by an arm around the neck from behind. Squeezing with the hands is much less effective and is relatively easy to dislodge.

The 'Judo strangle' or 'rear naked choke' taught by military instructors is highly effective for silent killing. One forearm goes around the neck of the opponent from behind, with the strangle locked in with the other arm. It is applied by pushing the opponent's head forward, essentially closing off the neck by compressing the operative's arm and the opponent's neck into the same space. If applied fast and hard a strangle of this sort can produce unconsciousness in 7-10 seconds and will kill soon afterwards.

A similar effect can be achieved with a rope or garrotte pulled around the neck, though it must be tight. If blood flow to the brain is reduced to an insufficient degree the target will be able to struggle and perhaps escape. To avoid this, the target should be pulled in close and held tightly to prevent escape or countermeasures.

In short, the key to close-quarters silent killing is to get the target under control and keep them like that until they are dead.

SPOT RULES FOR CHOKEHOLDS

 If an investigator has been trained in the use of chokeholds, the Keeper may allow him or her to attempt to take down an opponent in a single round. This involves performing a combat manoeuvre with an extra penalty die, to reflect the difficulty of targeting the carotid artery. If the attack is successful, the target must pass a Hard CON roll or fall unconscious for 1D6 rounds.

ASSASSINATION TECHNIQUES

Assassination differs from silent killing in that the primary goal is the death of the target. Obviously, there are times where an assassination must be performed silently, but when this is unnecessary there are various methods available. It is worth noting that if an assassination attempt fails, further opportunities are unlikely if the target or their security detail realise that an attempt has been made. Highly overt methods are somewhat all-or-nothing, whereas it may be possible to use a subtler method with a lesser chance of alerting the target if it fails.

SHOOT TO KILL

The simplest method of assassination is to shoot the target with a firearm. In theory, any gunshot wound can kill, so conventional wisdom suggests that a large-calibre rifle bullet might be the most efficient method. However, as distance increases so too do the variables. A long-range shot has only to be slightly off to be non-fatal or even to miss entirely. Ideally a circumstances must be created such that the target is stationary at a known point and therefore relatively easy to hit. A skilled spotter should be employed to observe the effects of a hit or to correct misses if there is time.

 A well-operated cell rarely attracts police interest and thus its leaders are not under investigation. This makes their sudden murder noteworthy, especially if they are believed to be upstanding members of their community. Remember that you need to maintain deniability. A few extra unaffiliated corpses may very well throw off the hounds.- Miller

The fundamental rule for firearms assassination is that close range increases the chance of success – but also the difficulty of obtaining the shot and escaping afterwards. If it is possible to shoot and disable the target then close in and deliver a coup de grace then this is an effective method. The next best thing is to shoot the target multiple times. A target that is not instantly killed may be saved by prompt medical attention; a group of shots not only increases the chance of an instant kill by striking a vital organ but also makes treating a non-fatal shooting more difficult.

Thus a small-calibre handgun or rapid-fire submachine gun may be the best choice for close range assassination. A group of small-calibre wounds close together are much more difficult to treat than a single larger-calibre one or a dispersed group. The low recoil of a small-calibre weapon will not move the aim point around much, ensuring accuracy and tight grouping. One technique for weapons of this sort

is rather unappetisingly called 'zippering'. A series of shots is 'walked' up the abdomen of the target so that they create a wide wound zone. This makes bleeding very difficult to control and virtually ensures death even if medical attention is swiftly received.

 Zippering, yeah, try and zipper something made of living flame and see where that gets you. Better still, zipper the bastard who called it, those who work for him and anyone who saw it. – Rodriquez

Zippering requires a weapon capable of multiple rapid shots, such as a semi-automatic pistol or a small-calibre revolver. A machine pistol, or a handgun capable of automatic fire, will serve admirably but may attract unwelcome attention. At longer ranges a similar effect can be achieved by using a larger submachine gun or an assault rifle. Dumping an entire magazine into the target is known in some quarters as a 'fast kill' and, whilst hardly elegant, it virtually guarantees rapid death.

SILENCE AND SURPRISE

The key here is to get close to the target and deliver the attack by surprise. Ideally the victim will know nothing of the threat until he is hit, though often there is no option but to deploy the weapon as the operative approaches which may alert guards or the target himself. It is the operative's ability to put themselves in position using stealth or deception that dictates the success or otherwise of the assassination attempt; skill with the weapon and the characteristics of the weapon itself are of lesser importance at close range.

A 'silent' weapon such as the Welrod pistol or the De Lisle carbine (both were used during World War Two but remain available) offers the advantage of not alerting guards or nearby non-combatants. It may be possible to kill the target whilst nobody is looking then move off before the alarm is raised. Weapons of this sort do not shoot quickly, but a target that is disabled by the first shot can be finished off with a second. It is sometimes more effective to shoot to disable with the first round, then to kill with the second – but only if there is little chance of guards being alerted.

It should however be noted that even 'silent' weapons are not without noise. A so-called 'silencer' (whether manufactured or improvised) fitted to a pistol or a submachine gun will greatly reduce the sound it makes but the shot will still be audible over a short distance. It may not be recognised as such, however, nor noticed through a wall or over background noise. It is also notable that working a pistol slide or the bolt of a larger weapon creates a distinctive sound that can seem surprisingly loud when there is no other noise; in the dead of night, for example.

 Steuben has been compromised. Take all necessary action. -N

If there is time for only one shot, then it must be perfectly placed to kill the target. This is often the case when using a sniper rifle or similar weapon, or with a weapon such as a pistol cartridge disguised in a lipstick container, a pen or a similar item. These are one-shot weapons, and while they are sometimes reloadable, the chance for assassination will be long gone by this time. These weapons must be used by surprise, either by stealth or distraction.

One potential drawback to such methods is their precision. A target that has been killed in their office by a close-range pistol shot suggests the actions of a skilled assassin; this may draw a determined response. It may sometimes be beneficial to make an assassination seem like the work of local criminals, political or business rivals, or perhaps someone the victim has offended in a serious manner.

Mobile Targets

It is relatively easy to secure a building by first checking it for explosives and hostiles and then flooding the grounds with guards, but high levels of security are less simple to maintain when the target is on the move.

Crowds offer an excellent opportunity to get close to the target, and random foot traffic in a public place offers a chance to blend in with background activity. There are many distractions in public, all of which can weaken a target's security their his own situational awareness. The random actions of people going about their business will often provide an opportunity for the assassin to approach the target even if the situation has not been manipulated to create one.

Similarly, vehicles present many opportunities for assassination. A vehicle can be rigged to malfunction or explode, though this first requires access to it. Such tampering can be detected by a security detail or an alert target, and is not always reliable.

Rigging a vehicle to malfunction is an uncertain method of assassination. A common method is to cause the brakes to fail, which has the added advantage of not being obviously assassination. However, brake failure can be survivable or the target may be extricated from the situation by skilful

driving. It is more difficult to tamper with steering or other vital vehicle functions.

A simple bomb wired into the ignition can be effective, but it can be triggered by the wrong person starting the vehicle. Command detonation is more assured, and offers two different methods of attack. The first is a bomb in the vehicle itself, which is detonated at a time of the operator's choosing. This requires access to the vehicle, and the end result is overt.

Equally obvious is the emplaced device, which is detonated when the target vehicle is within range of the bomb.

An emplaced device is only useful if the target's route is known; it is standard practice among bodyguard details to vary routes wherever possible and to maintain security about timing and route to be taken. This can make an emplaced bomb impractical.

The timing of a detonation is critical; even a small error can make an emplaced bomb survivable. One option is to use the target vehicle as a trigger, either when it comes into direct contact with the device or by timing its passage from a known point to the detonation site. Alternatively, if the target's escort vehicle always maintains an exact spacing, the escort can be used as a trigger.

Explosives can be used against a vehicle in other ways. An anti-tank rocket will obliterate most civilian vehicles, leaving no survivors. Alternatively, it may be possible to throw an explosive or incendiary device, or even a grenade, into the vehicle. Open-topped cars are most readily attacked in this manner.

A vehicle can be attacked with firearms. Something as simple as killing the driver can cause a fatal crash, though if it is possible to shoot the occupants of a vehicle then it will be more effective to engage the target directly. Getting a precise shot on a moving target is difficult, especially when firing from a moving vehicle too. Automatic weapons are most useful for such attacks; rifles are preferable as they have greater penetration than submachine guns; the frame of a car offers only a little protection to the occupants but sometimes is sufficient to impair lighter calibres.

Riddling the passenger compartment with automatic gunfire is crude but effective. It may also be useful to shoot out tyres, thereby causing loss of control. A crash may finish off wounded occupants and will certainly immobilise the vehicle, allowing a more precise finish to the attack or at least preventing the occupants from reaching assistance.

Similar considerations apply to aircraft and watercraft, with the added comment that both operate in an environment that can be hostile to human life. An aircraft that suffers a mechanical failure in flight can kill its occupants either by crashing or indirectly by stranding them in a remote area. A crash can be made to seem accidental, especially if weather conditions are already poor.

Similarly, boats do meet with disaster from time to time. If a wreck is not found then it may be impossible to prove that the disappearance was the result of foul play. There may also be doubt as to whether the target has been snatched, has defected or has simply been lost at sea.

As a general rule it is easier to assassinate a target away from official functions and workplace. Not only is the mindset of the target different when on 'home' territory or when away from work, but they are more likely to move freely and present opportunities that might otherwise be lacking. There is also the consideration that the places an official is likely to go on duty will have their own security measures in place. An assassination is best carried out somewhere that the operative will have only to contend with one set of security measures.

POISONS AND OTHER CHEMICALS

Chemical substances have a variety of uses in intelligence work, not all of them violent in intent.

Drugs, poisons and other agents need to get into the victim's bloodstream in order to work, and this occurs in four main ways:

· **Ingested agents** must enter the body through the digestive system, i.e. they must be eaten or drunk.

HANDLING ASSASSINATION ATTEMPTS

If an assassination attempt is made in a manner that is covered by the standard combat rules, then these can be used as normal. For example, if an operative attempts a drive-by shooting with a submachine gun then this is a fairly typical combat situation.

To be considered a special case an assassination attempt must come as a surprise to the target; the character must approach undetected or unsuspected and make the initial attack by surprise. This requires the use of other skills to deceive the target into not suspecting the assassin or causing them to fail to notice that he is there at all.

The actual attack will come at the end of a series of other actions required to facilitate it, and this may not be simple. It may be that a would-be assassin will jump through all manner of hoops to reach the target, only to find that they are at least partially alerted. In this case, the assassination attempt becomes regular combat. Players who get it right will find that a successful assassination is almost an anticlimax. Those who bull their way through may well fail completely.

Note that for an assassination attempt to take place, it is not necessary that the target be completely oblivious. For example, a false threat might cause the target to seek the safety of their vehicle, not realising that the 'bodyguard' holding the door open is the actual assassin. Although agitated and alerted, the target might still be taken by surprise by this unexpected threat. Similarly, a target who is looking towards a known threat can still be assassinated by someone who sneaks up behind them or shoots them in the back. In short, to be considered an assassination attempt the situation must deprive the target of any chance to make meaningful resistance or evasion during the initial attempt to kill them.

See pg. 137 of *World War Cthulhu: Cold War* for game mechanics covering assassination attempts.

HANDLING DRUGS, POISONS, TOXINS

 We roughly subdivide chemicals into drugs, poisons and toxins depending on their general effects. Medical textbooks may use a different set of definitions, but these will suffice for running a game of *World War Cthulhu*.

For our purposes, a POISON is any substance that is likely to cause severe harmful effects to the target if it is introduced. These effects include death or physical damage of a sort that can be modelled with the combat rules.

A TOXIN in this context is a substance that causes some other harmful effect such as temporary reduction in characteristics or skills.

All other substances that can affect a character are termed DRUGS for our purposes. Drugs include chemicals such as sodium pentathol, which is often used during interrogation; it does not cause harm to the target (or at least, that is not its main purpose), and so is not considered a poison or toxin. Most drugs can kill if administered in excessive doses or when combined with other chemicals, but are still considered drugs rather than poisons unless harming the target is the primary purpose.

We use the term AGENT as a catch-all in this context for any drug, toxin or poison that might be used by or against operatives. Agents can take many forms but are typically a gas, liquid or pill. In order to deliberately introduce an agent into someone's body it must be produced or converted into some form that permits this. For example, some poisons can be dissolved in liquid for delivery. It would be quite difficult to get an enemy operative to eat a packet of sedative powder, but dissolved in a glass of wine it becomes somewhat easier to deliver.

- **Injected agents** can be delivered by hypodermic needle. They can also be injected by other means, such as the fangs of a snake. It is not necessary for the injection to be neat and tidy; any method that breaks the skin will work, such as stabbing the target with a blunt pen whose nib contains a pellet of the agent. However, the aim is to get the agent into the bloodstream so that the target's own body functions carry it to his vital organs. Injection into a vein is most effective, whereas merely crushing the agent into an area of mangled skin might not be.

Inhaled agents generally take the form of a vapour but can be a toxic gas such as chlorine. Some gases are not actually harmful so much as they do not support respiration.

An opponent can be effectively drowned in carbon dioxide; they will not suffer any harm from the carbon dioxide itself, but will still die from lack of oxygen. Chlorine and other gases have additional harmful effects, such as causing blistering of the skin or lungs.

Contact agents can pose a hazard if they touch any bare skin. Many are more effective if they can come into contact with mucous membranes such as the eyes and mouth, and even more so if breathed in.

 Poisons are rarely of use against Our Other Enemy, and their use against their servants is not recommended. A poisoned target is likely to end up in a hospital before they end up dead, either taken there by an accomplice or a bystander. Even if the target is left alone to die, poisoning is likely to bring official interest, something we cannot afford. Considering the lengths needed to effectively poison someone and the risks entailed, more direct means are desirable. -N

Protection against different agents depends upon their mode of use. Ingested agents require food or drink to be consumed injected agents must be conveyed to the bloodstream by a penetrating injury or a needle. Avoiding intoxication by these agents is a matter of being careful with what food and drink is accepted and maintaining good personal security. The most likely scenario for an operative to be injected with a chemical agent is after capture, through it could occur in a situation where they have let their guard down inappropriately.

Contact and inhaled agents are defeated by avoiding contact with the agent or preventing it from coming into contact with respiratory surfaces. A purely respiratory agent can be defeated by a respirator or other breathing device, though many (such as tear gas) can affect the victim by contact with mucous membranes in the eyes. Nerve gases can be defeated only by complete impermeable coverage of the body (in an NBC suit) and a gas mask or similar device sealed to the suit. However, partial protection is possible by covering as much skin as possible and breathing through a cloth or filter. This will not work in the middle of a gas cloud but where the agent is somewhat dispersed these measures will give the operative a chance of survival.

Ultimately, whether or not the victim is affected by an agent depends on the severity of intoxication and their natural resistance. If an agent is kept completely 'out' of the target, such as when an attempt to inject them fails, then they cannot be affected at all. If they are exposed to the agent, they may still resist its effects. Note that not all agents have an immediate effect. Some cause secondary effects that can take hours or even days to become apparent.

TYPES OF DRUGS, POISONS AND PATHOGENS

There are a great many agents that an operative might be exposed to. Most are chemically derived, but some of those below are of a biological nature. This section also contains some notes on radiation and fallout which may be relevant to certain situations.

DAMAGE AND OTHER EFFECTS FROM CHEMICAL AGENTS

The effects of most toxins can be modelled using the rules found on pg. 129 of the *Call of Cthulhu rulebook*. In these cases, the toxin causes damage that is healed as normal. Indeed, some agents (snake venom, for example) cause physical damage to the area around the site of intoxication. Some poisons are instantly fatal, and may or may not have other effects if the victim survives. For example, someone who resists a potentially fatal toxin may suffer from blurred vision, headache and nausea for some time afterwards, or may take physical damage that could end up being fatal in its own right. Other agents have different effects which may not be directly fatal but which can impair an investigator to the point where they are taken out by some secondary cause.

Depending on circumstances, the Keeper may wish to call for CON rolls from poisoned investigators to determine how badly incapacitated they are by pain, delirium or paralysis; failure could lead to all rolls being made at a higher level of difficulty (Regular becomes Hard, Hard becomes Extreme), or with a penalty die if opposed, until the investigator receives an antidote or medical help. This is especially appropriate for psychoactive agents or soporifics that may not inflict physical damage.

Bacterial Agents make use of bacteria that grow and multiply in the host. Effects vary considerably, and although many agents are resistant to antibiotics some specialist treatments do exist. Bacterial agents can be difficult to weaponise; in other ways, whilst it is easy to culture the deadly bacteria, creating reliable means of delivery is a problem.

The most well-known bacterial agent is anthrax, which causes flu-like symptoms that can (but do not always) kill if spores are inhaled. Like most bacterial agents, anthrax has an incubation period before symptoms present themselves (1-6 days in this case). Respiratory and skin contact protection are both required to avoid infection.

Biological Toxins are similar to chemical toxins except that they are derived more or less directly from living organisms. The toxins are not alive and cannot be transmitted, but in some cases the organism creating them can.

Examples include botulinum (which causes respiratory failure some 36 hours after an incubation period of 24-26 hours) and aflatoxin, which is a toxin derived from fungi. Aflatoxin causes rapid kidney failure and death, and can be passed on to others who come into contact with fluids from the victim. Ricin is of particular interest to the intelligence community since it can be delivered by almost any means. After ingestion or inhalation it incubates for 12-24 hours before causing death after another 36-72 hours. Ricin poisoning produces symptoms that can easily be mistaken for a viral infection.

Blister Agents cause coughing and respiratory distress in addition to severe irritation of the eyes. Many, such as lewisite and mustard gas, also create what appear to be corrosive burns on the skin. These do not usually appear for some hours after exposure, and can occur when moving through a contaminated area even though no other effects have been noted – contamination is quite persistent. Blister agents are simple to manufacture and may be encountered when operating in remote Third World countries where enforcement of international treaties is unheard of. NBC suiting will prevent skin effects, whilst respiratory protection is required when the agent is present in gas form.

Blood Agents include cyanide and prevent absorption of oxygen into the blood. Low doses manifest symptoms within an hour or two of exposure, including deep and rapid breathing, dizziness and similar symptoms of deoxygenation. Higher doses cause rapid unconsciousness and death. Exposure is usually by inhalation, but intoxication can take place by way of cuts in the skin. Cyanide pills are often used as suicide devices.

Chemical Incapacitants, including mace, pepper spray and tear gas, irritate the airways and mucous membranes of the eyes and nose. This causes coughing, eye irritation and vomiting in most targets, and can be fatal in very high concentrations. Contact with the irritant is enough to produce an effect, whilst breathing it has the greatest impact. Partial protection is possible with nothing more than a cloth held over the mouth and nose, especially where the agent is highly dispersed.

Choking Agents include gases such as phosgene and chlorine, which damage the respiratory tract. Onset of symptoms may be slow, taking anything from 30 minutes to more than 24 hours. Death occurs as a result of fluid build-up in the lungs. Exposure can be prevented by respiratory protection such as a gas mask.

Nerve Agents include various 'nerve gases' such as sarin, soman and tabun. These are formed by a liquid that evaporates to create a lethal gas. Minor doses can be non-fatal, though sometimes still cause long-term effects. Mildly intoxicated casualties are often disorientated and have difficulty in thinking clearly. Fatal doses result in convulsions and respiratory failure. Skin contact can be fatal but requires a stronger dose than inhalation; the only sure protection is full NBC suiting followed by proper decontamination.

Plagues sometimes forms the basis of a biological weapon, but can also be a natural threat in some regions. Plagues are bacterial in nature and are hard to control once released; this makes their use by most nations somewhat unlikely, although some terrorist groups might consider their use. Bubonic plague, which caused the Black Death, is difficult to weaponised but it believed that the Soviet Union may have done so. A pneumonic form of plague can be dispersed by aerosol and represents a greater threat, although exposure to sunlight will kill it in a few hours. This form of plague has an incubation period of 2-3 days followed by high fever leading to death from respiratory and circulatory collapse. Infection can be avoided by normal medical protection: gowns, masks and gloves, or the equivalent.

Psychoactive Agents range from gases such as BZ to chemicals such as LSD. BZ can be delivered in gas form – BZ gas grenades exist – and can incapacitate targets through confusion, hallucinations or stupor. Side-effects can continue for weeks after exposure. Respiratory protection is necessary. Chemicals such as LSD have no military value as they are hard to weaponised – delivery is usually by ingestion or injection – but can be useful in interrogation. Threats have been made by various nations to use psychoactive chemicals against military or civilian targets, but no known attacks have occurred.

A Note About Chemical and Biological Weapons

Dying of plague or anthrax is hardly the stuff of fun gaming sessions. We do suggest that the information given here be used as part of the background rather than a new and not very exciting way to kill off investigators. A biological or chemical threat might be part of the backdrop to a mission or a complication to one; for example, having to operate in a contaminated area.

That said, we have included information on these threats for the Keeper to make whatever use of they see fit. If investigators ignore the warnings then maybe they will die of a perfectly mundane haemorrhagic fever instead of the arcane horrors they are battling. Nobody said the job was safe...

Soporifics come in various forms including gases, vapours and ingested chemicals. The latter may be a pill or 'knockout drop', or a powder that can be dissolved in liquid. Ether or chloroform vapour will also render the victim unconscious. An excessive dose of any soporific can be fatal. Some chemicals do not render the victim unconscious but can cause a tranquil state in which the subject does not care about discomfort or even pain, and is often highly suggestible. It is usually obvious that the subject is under the influence of tranquillisers of this sort; at the very least they will behave strangely and may seem drunk or high.

Viral Agents are essentially normal viral diseases employed as a weapon. Like bacterial agents and plagues, they are difficult to control once released and can mutate, making their use as a weapon inadvisable. Protection against viral agents is the same as for other diseases; contact should be avoided with infected people or animals. However, the incubation period of vital diseases may allow infected persons to contact many potential victims.

Examples of viral agents include Ebola and other viral haemorrhagic fevers, many of which are not carried by humans. Infection must be by contact with an infected animal or deliberate means, but once infected a person can pass on the virus by contact with blood and body fluids. The most serious viral threat is smallpox, which has an incubation period of 10-17 days and about 30% fatal thereafter. Natural outbreaks of smallpox still occur from time to time, but the disease is all but eradicated in the natural world. It is highly transmissible, and would make a potent if indiscriminate biological weapon.

Radiation and Radioactivity are neither chemical nor biological threats, but are similar in some ways, especially since many radioactive materials are also highly toxic. There are two primary threats from radioactivity. The first is direct exposure to intense radiation in the form of gamma rays. These penetrate flesh and most other materials. A radiation suit offers a little protection but it is not possible to enter a high-radiation area without being contaminated. The body can withstand a certain amount of radiation without coming to harm, and more with only mild or long-term effects. Severe radiation poisoning is fatal and untreatable. The only sure protection is thick earth or metal.

The second threat from radioactivity comes from exposure to radioactive materials emitting alpha and beta radiation. These are short-ranged and easily blocked by thin metal or even paper, but highly damaging, especially if inhaled or ingested.

An NBC suit or similar protection will prevent most effects if suitably decontaminated; in the case of moderate exposure the threat can be greatly reduced by disposing of clothing and washing all dust or other material off the skin. It is imperative to avoid breathing or eating food contaminated by radioactive material, such as fallout from a nuclear explosion.

DISPOSING OF BODIES AND OTHER EVIDENCE

Operatives who leave evidence of their activities lying around are likely to be discovered, especially if that evidence consists of human corpses. There are times, for example during a 'fast and quiet' entry to a locale, when guards must be dropped where they are found and left there. This is particularly true where a guard in an inaccessible place is shot by a sniper to clear the way for an entry team. However, wherever possible any and all evidence of an operative's activities should be concealed or removed entirely.

In the longer term, evidence such as cartridge cases left at an operational locale can lead the enemy's intelligence services to the operative. Basic errors like failing to remove wrappers and half-eaten food from a location used for surveillance can give the enemy good information to go on. Clean-up of all operational locales should be a habit for all operatives. This includes removing fingerprints from any items touched and disposing of any rubbish such as papers, food wrappers and the like in a manner that ensures they will not be found, or at least so as to be of no use to the enemy.

CLEANING UP OPERATIONAL LOCALES

 If there is a chance that a location used by the investigators will come under scrutiny by the police, counterintelligence services or other interested professionals, the Keeper should have one member of the team make a combined Stealth and Tradecraft roll. Failure could mean that the team have left suspicious traces, and a fumble or failed pushed roll that they have missed some item that will make it possible to trace or identify them.

For mundane waste such as food or a newspaper used as a disguise prop, it may well be sufficient to dispose of items in the same manner as any other waste, using normal amenities. Items will be lost amid all the other waste and will soon be gone forever. However, disposal should be at a distance from the operational locale; hostile intelligence services may search every bin within a considerable distance from the scene.

 You might think that fire is a good means to cleanse a site after all the hard work is done. The Boss doesn't think so, but he tends to be a bit more cautious these days. Look, fire wipes out those bloodstains, scrawled runes, ancient tomes and a lot of esoteric brick-a-brac. It also hides bodies nicely; at least in the manner we need to hide them. Despite what the fire marshal says on the witness stand, fire science is not that accurate, and the coroner is less likely to look over charred remains as closely as a fresh, clean corpse. – Rodriguez

For more incriminating items, such as cartridge cases or guns, greater care is needed. Items of this sort can be concealed in a basic manner, for example wrapping them in a bag, and then placed in a bin along with other rubbish, but this should only be done if the operative needs to get rid of the items in a great hurry.

Rivers and other bodies of water offer a good way to get rid of guns and similar items; the chances of one being found are low providing disposal is not near to the operational locale. It may be useful to handoff an incriminating weapon to another operative tasked with disposal; providing the handoff is not observed the chances of interception before disposal are greatly reduced.

Even if a weapon cannot be traced back to the user, much can be learned from it or from casings left at the scene of a shooting. One solution is to use a revolver or bolt-action weapon, so that cases stay in the weapon until the operative extracts them; semi- and fully-automatic weapons fling cases out during the reloading cycle which can make them hard to recover quickly, or at all.

If the operative is forced to kill someone, the body must be disposed of unless the intent is for it to be found. Transporting a body is risky, and disposal can cause problems. Extremely hot and sustained fire will destroy a corpse, but otherwise it may be best to bury it somewhere remote. Other items can also be buried if no better means of disposal is available. Providing the site is carefully chosen and the operative is unobserved, discovery should be unlikely.

However, any place an operative can get to with a body without taking so long about it that they attract attention is a place that others might go. Eventually undergrowth will hide a burial site, and this process can be speeded up by careful concealment, but a fresh burial is quite easy to spot even by a random passer-by. Disposal of items, bodies and such like must be permanent. Once disposal has taken place the operative should never go back in case he leads the enemy to the site. It may be tempting to check that a disposal has not been discovered; this is too risky.

 Disposal of inhuman remains is a difficult process. Often, they rather thankfully take care of that themselves, dissolving into nothingness and leaving little to clean up. When they do not, you run two risks. First, even dead their forms are shocking and dangerous, sometimes merely to one's mental health, other times they are toxic in some manner. Second, and possibly the more important, risk is that of discovery. Even the bones of the more-humanoid creatures do not

appear human in the least, and if discovered can easily lead to too many questions being asked by the wrong people. -N

 Industrial solvents. You can buy them at speciality stores with the right permits, and you can fake those permits pretty easy. Me, I like to dump things that should never be found into a foundry. Except Deep Ones: I send those back into the sea. - Miller

In the context of the mission at hand, disposal of bodies and other incriminating items may be impossible. If an operative or team is moving fast, it may not be possible to conceal any evidence of their passage. However, as noted elsewhere, as soon as bodies start to drop, the countdown to discovery begins. It can be slowed by concealing evidence, such as by dragging bodies out of sight.

It will rarely be possible to sanitise the site of a kill; there is likely to be blood or other evidence of the act, but a bloodstain is less likely to be spotted than a corpse lying around, especially at night. As a simple rule, the more imminent completion of a mission is, the less care need be taken about concealing bodies. For example, if a driver is killed for his uniform on the day of the operation, it is vital that the body is not discovered in time to raise the alarm or else the mission will be blown from the start. A guard eliminated at the front gates of an assassination target's residence must not be discovered until the assassins are close enough to strike. The amount of care taken to conceal the killing must match the length of time it needs to remain undiscovered.

Of course, in an ideal mission the enemy should not realise anything has happened until the operatives are long gone, if they ever know for certain that an operation took place. However, at the very least bodies and other obvious signs that something is happening must be concealed until the operation is over if the operatives want to make a clean exit.

This may be more difficult than it sounds. A corpse is not only heavy, but is extremely awkward to move and may leave a blood trail in doing so. Objects can fall out of pockets and hands, leaving clues for alert guards to pick up on. The best hiding places for bodies are inside something such as a car or cupboard, but operatives must be aware that a corpse may continue to bleed and give its position away in this manner.

A corpse can be dragged out of sight to hide it from casual glances. Concealment of this sort can be enhanced by covering it or otherwise breaking up the distinctive outline of a human body. A shapeless clump of shadows may not pique the interest of a passing guard on a rainy night, but a leg sticking out of a clump of bushes certainly will. What cannot be completely hidden can be camouflaged by simple expedients like draping a dark blanket or curtain over it.

It should be noted that under most circumstances it is better not to kill anyone at all. If guards and other personnel can be misdirected, bribed or otherwise bypassed then less evidence is left behind of an intelligence operation and the response may be lower-key than if a team of operatives blasts its way through the opposition to carry out its mission.

HANDLING THE DISPOSAL OF BODIES

Hiding a body quickly requires a combination of skill, strength and luck. In situations where the investigators are under time pressure, or there is a significant risk of discovery, the Keeper should call for a combined STR, Luck and Spot Hidden roll. This covers the process of identifying a suitable hiding place, dragging the body into position and not leaving obvious blood stains or other trails in the process.

If there is time to dispose of a body methodically, the Keeper may call for a combined Stealth and Tradecraft roll to remove all traces of what has happened. This is only required if the site of the kill is likely to come under scrutiny, or if the Keeper simply wants to make the players nervous.

If the investigator needs to make it difficult to identify a body by cutting off hands or fingers, pulling teeth or removing the head, and they have never done so before, the Keeper may call for a Sanity roll (0/1D6). Investigators who have experience of this kind of work are assumed to have become at least partially inured; the Keeper may still call for a Sanity roll, but this should only be for colour, reflecting how reluctant the investigator is, or whether the process makes them vomit.

I, I need to be picked up.

The two men the Guvnor sent answered the codewords, but I didn't, didn't recognise them. They had human faces, but anyone can wear one of those!

I told them to unmask, but they just looked at me with those empty, empty glass eyes.

GET, GET ME OUT OF HERE. DON'T BREATHE; BREATH, THE SHADOWS SEE.

The Guvnor, the Guvnor has been compromised. - Stanton

CHAPTER SIX
COVERT OPERATIONS

·COVERT OPERATIONS·

The term 'covert operation' is used in this chapter to refer to operations that go beyond the bounds of typical espionage and counter-espionage missions. Whilst a burglary to obtain documents or a kidnapping of a foreign scientist might fall under the heading of covert operations, these tend to be low-key missions that do not involve anyone outside our own intelligence services and support agencies. The following sections deal with situations where personnel must operate alongside local rebels and dissidents, or must engage in more direct methods including direct (but deniable) armed confrontation.

OPERATING ALONGSIDE LOCAL INSURGENTS, DISSIDENTS AND REVOLUTIONARIES

The enemy of your enemy is not your friend. He is a co-belligerent; he is hostile to your enemy, but that says nothing about his attitude towards you. In some cases, warm and close relationships can be formed with local insurgent or dissident groups, and some may genuinely be our friends in either a personal or political sense. But to assume this relationship exists simply because of a shared enemy is dangerous.

Some co-belligerents have their own agenda and some hate us as much as the common enemy. There is no guarantee that they will not turn on us due to their own internal politics or because our aims diverge from theirs. Similarly, some groups are sufficiently corrupt that they will sell out our operatives or change sides for gain, and even within a truly friendly group there may be individuals who will do so given the right circumstances. Our intelligence operatives actively make use of this possibility; it stands to reason that the opposition will too.

Even within a closely allied group, the nature of their hostility to our enemy may differ from ours, and some of their personnel may be inclined to act in a way that compromises our goals. We can, as a rule, control our own people but there is no guarantee that a local revolutionary working with us can or will do so. Caution must always be exercised when working with locals, not least since the possibility exists that they are playing both sides off against the other or are seeking to gain from the situation. Even if it is obvious to us that cooperation is in the common interest this does not mean that someone else will see it the same way, no matter what they have said or done in the past.

Our Other Enemy is Our Other Enemy; this does not mean that other foes are not enemies. While it may be acceptable to work with them to defeat a greater evil, do not at any point assume that someone on the other side of the line is your ally. Even if they are one of us, you and they should treat each other as assets, to be used and disposed of as necessary for a greater good. -N

Therefore, any cooperation with local insurgents, dissidents or revolutionaries must be tackled with caution and care so as not to 'go native' (see pg. 28). Cut-outs are necessary to reduce the damage if locals betray our operatives, and we must be careful only to share information that is necessary. That said, it is possible to sour relations with local groups by seeming not to trust them, so cooperation must be (or seem to be) sufficiently wholehearted as to satisfy the locals about our intentions and relations with them.

In other words, local groups are to be used rather than treated as friends. If it is in our long-term interests to make sacrifices on their behalf then it is acceptable to do so; as a rule we want locals to do our dirty work for us and to take the consequences of our actions. This is harsh, but necessary. These are not our people, and quite likely not our friends in the long term either.

Operating with individuals and small groups is discussed in **Chapter Two: Networks and Assets**; the situation is slightly different when working with larger groups. It is possible to evaluate assets on an individual basis and form an opinion of their reliability. This is not usually possible with groups; operates tend to deal only with part of the group and cannot assess individuals from a fleeting contact.

INSURGENTS, REVOLUTIONARIES AND DISSIDENTS

Local groups can be divided into different categories based on their capabilities and attitudes towards us and the opposition: insurgents, revolutionaries and dissidents.

Insurgents are actively engaged in fighting against the opposition, usually by means of an urban or rural guerrilla war. Whilst this is often aimed at an eventual change of government, we draw a distinction between insurgents (who are actively using military means, albeit perhaps on a small scale) and other types of opposition groups.

Revolutionaries are actively seeking the overthrow of a government and (usually, but not always) its replacement with a more acceptable regime – acceptable to them, that is, not necessarily to us. We consider a revolutionary to become an insurgent when they engage in open warfare. This can happen for a variety of reasons, and almost always ensues following a failed coup.

Revolutionaries may be willing to fight as insurgents or may prefer to use other means. These can include legal and constitutional methods, often with a mixture of illegal activity. For example a revolutionary group might be unwilling to engage in warfare but find coercing judges to rule in the manner they are directed entirely acceptable. Revolutionaries can come from within a regime, such as a clique of army officers who wish to form a junta, or may represent a disaffected segment of the populace.

Dissidents are unhappy with the opposition and often prepared to cause low-level trouble – perhaps including rioting – but do not engage in military action and are not usually intent on replacing the government. Dissidents can range from politicised workers or students to a segment

of an unhappy population. Most dissident groups are not very extreme – for example many intellectuals are willing to go no further than writing a particularly nasty pamphlet on governmental wrongdoings – but within their ranks can often be found potential assets or individuals willing to go to extreme lengths.

DEALING WITH DISSIDENT GROUPS

Reading, understanding and manipulating people can be a matter of life or death to an intelligence officer. This is especially true when dealing with groups of insurgents, dissidents and guerrillas. The problem is that dealing with such groups presents many potential difficulties.

The Keeper should use the following guidelines for adjusting Psychology rolls to read a group of guerrillas or interpersonal skill rolls for attempting to convince or manipulate them.

One penalty die for each of:

- The investigators have to work through an interpreter.
- The group has no defined leader.
- The group is from a country that has historical reasons to distrust Western powers.
- The group receives material support from the Soviets.

One bonus die for each of:

- The group are ideologically opposed to the investigators' enemies.
- The investigators are providing material aid.
- The investigators are working with good intelligence about the group's goals and ideologies.

Dissidents often have no real agenda beyond protesting about conditions they find unfair or unacceptable. They must be approached with caution; someone who is unhappy at their own government may still be loyal to it when the alternative is working with a foreign intelligence service.

It should be noted that many dissident groups are ineffectual. Membership may be more of a fashion accessory for 'revolutionary-chic' individuals than a statement of actual intent. Indeed, many of these pseudo-revolutionaries would be horrified at the thought of doing more than talking about overthrowing the government and might actually warn the authorities rather than allow an operation that might upset the local apple cart.

Dissident groups are often heavily infiltrated by police and intelligence agency informers, and may be highly disorganised. Their internal politics can be quite vigorous, with some members seeking direct and violent action (or shouting about it a lot for the sake of status within the group) and others urging a more patient and subtle (or ineffectual) approach.

Neutral Groups

Neutral groups might not share our enemy, but they can still prove useful to us. For example, a crime cartel might be able to obtain equipment or move personnel on our behalf, but are doing it for their own reasons – typically profit. Relations with a neutral group are often more of a business arrangement than a political alliance, but given the circumstances under which we operate such relationships can prove hazardous.

Motivations and Methodology

It is important to understand the motivations of any given group; what they might be willing to do and why. Dissidents will not respond well to calls to attack our opponents and might disown or even betray operatives if they go too far.

Nor are they likely to be receptive to offers of arms and military equipment in the same way that an insurgent group would. Similarly, workers' groups are likely to respond to different approaches to intellectuals and students, and have the capability to disrupt the enemy in different ways.

As a rule, it is best to quietly supply information and support to dissidents and revolutionaries, and hardware to insurgents; and then to exploit the harm they do to the opposition rather than try to precisely dictate what they do or relying on specific actions. Individuals within a group can be run as assets and may be trustworthy or reliable, but a group as a whole should be considered neither.

 You might get the idea of working with one cell of cattle against another; this is a very bad idea. If you think working

alongside a group of counter-insurgents is hairy, try it when the guy next to you is twitching away to his own visions. – Miller

Any group can move in either direction along the spectrum between mildly disaffected and fanatical revolutionary, and it is possible for a group as a whole to progress from dissidents to revolutionaries or insurgents, and vice versa.

This process can be manipulated by operatives who support the right people and provide information (true or otherwise) that pushes the group in the desired direction. There are times when destabilisation is desirable and others when we would prefer stability and peace. It may or may not be possible to ask groups to take the desired action, but it is always possible to manipulate them in the right direction – or at least to try.

TRUST AND GUERILLA GROUPS

 The Trust mechanic comes into play when an investigator is a member of a particular organisation or has strong ties with them. If an investigator is simply supporting a guerilla group or using them to achieve a particular objective, Trust is rarely a factor. If the investigator is trying to infiltrate the group or build a long-term working relationship with them, however, Trust becomes more important. Refer to *Building Trust* on pg. 48 of *World War Cthulhu: Cold War* for details.

OPERATING ALONGSIDE COMBAT TROOPS

At time, operatives will be required to operate alongside our own or allied armed forces. In some situations this may be overt cooperation, such as when intelligence agency personnel assist combat troops or accompany them on a mission. Cooperation may or may not be deniable; operational orders will cover how to relate to combat troops and how much information is to be divulged.

Our own troops and those of allied nations are not the enemy of our enemy; they are our friends. However, that does not make them trustworthy. US personnel currently serving in Vietnam, for example, may be demoralised conscripts who do not want anything to do with intelligence operations for the simple reason that they are dangerous and often 'dirty'. Disaffected and demoralise troops may not see the point of the mission and may not care about it. Mistrust is likely, and is probably well grounded as we do not routinely reveal operational details to those who do not need them.

Care must be taken not to place too much faith in regular troops; the holds true for civilian law enforcement personnel. Most are dedicated – or at least willing – to do their duty, but they do not see the big picture as we do, and may not be pleased to be put in danger for a vague or nebulous reason. Regular soldiers and law enforcement personnel may also lack critical skills and more importantly mindset. They may hesitate from taking 'dishonourable' but necessary actions, and may actually derail a mission by refusing orders or arguing at a time when action is critical.

 By far the biggest problem when operating alongside common soldiers is security. They cannot know about Our Other Enemy, yet there are times when you need to operate alongside them in order to carry out your mission. It is a cold calculation, but sometimes you have to expose them to psychological danger in order to get the job done, and clean up the mess afterwards. – Rodriquez

That said, these people also serve and must not be regarded with contempt or condescension. It may, however, be necessary under extreme circumstances to sacrifice or even betray them. We must never do this lightly, but there are times when the mission is more important than the survival of an assigned escort force. Hard choices must be made at times, but wherever possible allied and assigned forces must be treated fairly and accommodated as far as our mission and standing orders permit.

 Cold calculations are our business, and if you must feed an entire platoon into the maw to advance our fight, do so, and do so without remorse. -N

 This applies to us as well. – Steuben

Operations alongside regular troops or ordinary law enforcement personnel are not uncommon for some intelligence services in some parts of the world, but it is more likely that any combat personnel involved in our missions will be drawn from elite formations within the military and law enforcement world. These personnel share a mindset closer to ours and are both highly trained and

very motivated. Their methods tend to be more direct but they are 'our kind of people' in a way that regular soldiers are not.

Elite covert-operations personnel may be mistrustful of intelligence operatives, but as a rule they are mistrustful of anyone who has not earned their confidence. They are skilled at combat but have far greater capabilities than this; stealth, misdirection and specialist skills such as communications and use of explosives are all likely part of their training.

Many teams of elite forces are experts at winning over the local population; they may speak local languages and know customs that will gain them friends within the population.

The same skills are useful in an urban environment but this is more our province. It is rare for elite combat troops to be assigned to an intelligence operation other perhaps than in a specialist role as communicators, snipers or an assault team. Few elite operators are trained for the sort of long-term undercover work that intelligence personnel carry out.

Overall, when working with combat troops or law enforcement personnel, the general rule is that ordinary police and soldiers can only be trusted with routine tasks, whereas elite forces can be briefed on their part in the operation and allowed to see to the details from their own formidable skill set.

The most important distinction, however, is that elite operators live in the same world as we do and understand the hard choices that must sometimes be made. They can be relied upon in a way that ordinary combat personnel simply cannot. However, their worldview is still that of the warrior, and differs from that of an intelligence operative. Applied correctly, these differing mindsets and skill sets can be a powerful combination.

 One of the problems when dealing with the military is that they tend to favour a military approach to problem solving. Our Other Enemy tends to be resistant to the direct application of force. This is one of the many reasons we do not involve the military in our efforts, and you should keep this in mind when in the field. The right man at the right place at the right time can do more good than a thousand bullets and bombs ever could. -N

COVERT OPERATIONS SPECIALISTS AS INVESTIGATORS

 Depending on the nature of the scenario or campaign, the investigators may regularly be working alongside covert operations specialists. An intelligence officer from SIS, for example, may rely heavily on the Special Air Service (SAS) for certain missions.

If such personnel are going to play regular parts of your game, there is no reason not to make them investigators. A player may choose to swap between an intelligence officer and a covert operations specialist for different parts of the campaign, as appropriate. On some occasions, the Keeper may choose to have the players switch over to playing an entire team of covert operations specialists to carry out a hostage rescue, counter-terrorism operation or similar, then go back to playing their usual intelligence officers to deal with the aftermath.

Covert operations specialists can be created using the normal investigator creation rules in *World War Cthulhu: Cold War*. If the investigator has a previous occupation in the military and specialised training as a covert actions operative, they can be created with the appropriate set of skills.

SABOTAGE AND DISRUPTION

Sabotage, on a fairly small scale, can be the primary objective of a mission or may be a means to an end. For example, sabotage of an important machine or device could draw out a human target: maybe the key engineer whose task is to keep the machine running, or a specialist scientist sent to troubleshoot a programme. These personnel will then be more vulnerable to assassination or kidnapping.

 It might be hard to locate that cell leader, stop a tome from changing hands, or otherwise quietly disrupt a cell attempting

a major contact with Our Other Enemy. You know, they often have a set location and time they must do this thing in, a time and place open to sabotage.
– Rodriquez

Similarly, sabotage can be used to aid reconnaissance, enabling operatives to see how the enemy responds and who they send to deal with the problem. However, under most circumstances the sort of sabotage that can be undertaken by operatives will be of limited strategic value and may well represent an unnecessary risk of personnel in return for a very small gain.

Conversely, sabotage of a specific capability can be critical enough to merit an entire operation.

By way of example, a nation that has built a fast breeder nuclear reactor may be able to produce materials for use in nuclear weapons. Sabotaging the building or operation of such a reactor could set their nuclear programme back years. In this context, personnel can be considered a component of the programme; sabotaging it may require the elimination or removal of key personnel.

Sabotage on a small scale, such as disabling a machine in a factory for a day or two, is rarely worth the risk to an operative. Such minor sabotage, if it is done at all, is best carried out second or third hand by disaffected locals or rebels recruited and by the operative. Even then, it is unlikely to be worthwhile unless the production that is being disrupted is extremely high-value or difficult to replace locally. Slowing down the only machine for 300 miles capable of producing a precision component is potentially worthwhile; the tiny reduction in a nation's industrial output is not.

Sabotage of industrial production needs to be large-scale in order to be useful to our cause. This can be accomplished by various means that have little to do with machine-breaking. One option is to sow discontent among workers and foment labour disputes.

Passive resistance and 'slow working' proved effective during the World War Two when practised by workers in occupied countries; a similar situation exists in nations that have been forced to accept communism or where an unpopular dictator or junta is in place.

In such a case, there may be no need to actually damage anything; indeed this might be counterproductive. If a workers' go-slow appears to have no outside cause, this will probably cause more disruption over time than violently crippling a vital piece of machinery; the latter will probably bring about a more robust response than the former. A workers' dispute might even cause more widespread problems for the target if it grows into a general strike.

If workers can be induced to cause actual damage to their equipment, or local saboteurs can be persuaded to take direct action, they will need to know what to target and how. Indiscriminate damage may not be the best option; operatives should ensure that saboteurs attack the most critical components of a local industrial system or those that will cause the greatest destruction in the long term. If a shortage of a certain part can be identified then machines that require it are better targets than a critical

piece of equipment for which a good set of spares is always maintained.

Sabotage can also be accomplished through political and financial means as well as by direct action. Supply of raw materials can be disrupted by blowing up a bridge on the delivery route, but this has a shorter-term effect than blackmailing a raw material supplier into accepting contracts from other project, or engineering a dispute with local hauliers who carry raw materials to and from the plant. Likewise, shipping and rail infrastructure can be disrupted directly in the short term, but it may be far more effective to persuade the crane operators' union that they are being swindled by their employers.

Sabotage might also be carried out for political ends. For example, if a flagship government project fails to reach the targets that were loudly trumpeted at its inception, this can damage the opposing government. Disruption of electricity supplies or necessary goods to a population centre makes the local government seem weak and ineffectual even if it has little impact on industrial production.

Sabotage on a small scale might be carried out by operatives to facilitate a mission. For example, a vehicle might be sabotaged, or a mechanism operating a swinging or lifting bridge, to trap a target in the kill zone. However, a general sabotage campaign is best carried out by local dissidents who have been given some training in what to do and how to go about it.

If the goal is the long-term weakening of foreign industrial and economic production, with the associated political damage, then a low-key sabotage campaign best suits our purposes. It is better for production to be slowed by 'accidents', disputes and unavailability of raw materials or parts for machines that unaccountably keep breaking down, than by overt and dramatic action. The latter is more useful

MECHANICAL SABOTAGE

If an investigator wishes to disable an item of machinery in a hurry, and does not care about covering their tracks, then the Keeper can call for a Luck or Mechanical Repair (or Electrical Repair if there is a lot of wiring) roll to cover a brute-force approach such as dropping a spanner in the works. If the machinery is particularly complex or has exposed workings, this may afford the investigator a bonus die.

Should the investigator wish to make the damage look accidental, the roll becomes Hard; alternatively, the Keeper may ask for a combined Mechanical Repair and Tradecraft roll for the investigator to cover their tracks.

if an area is on the brink of major unrest or revolution, since highly obvious actions can encourage further attacks.

 Timing can be key, disrupt their time table and you can throw the whole thing off for days or weeks, giving you time to get the job done right. If the stars are right, make 'em wrong. – Miller

The sort of sabotage we encourage should therefore be tailored to the ends we wish to accomplish. Big, graphic actions can be part of a destabilisation campaign but are actually less damaging than ongoing low-key sabotage. Of course, creating the right conditions for a sabotage campaign conducted at third hand may require various missions to obtain documents, coerce individuals or otherwise manipulate the target group into acting on our behalf. Slow and subtle impairs the opposition in the long term; big and noisy is more properly used for political ends such as making the government seem ineffectual or triggering further unrest.

GUERRILLA WARFARE

Historically, guerrilla warfare has always been the province of a weaker power against a stronger one. It takes little more than a cause and a weapon to be a guerrilla fighter, but to be effective is a more difficult proposition. It is worth noting that although the terms are often confused, guerrillas and terrorists are two different things. A terrorist uses fear for political ends, often striking at civilian targets, whereas a guerrilla is fighting a war and will attack militarily valuable targets. Of course, the key to winning is to attack the enemy where they are weak, and it is possible to stray over the line from guerrilla warfare into terrorism, but they are not intrinsically the same.

 It is important to know the ideology of the guerrillas you are working with, if for no other reason to make the relationship proceed without any disruptions. However, if you can manipulate a small force to perform the heavy lifting for an otherwise quiet mission, and can rely on them to succeed, there is no reason to use this relationship towards your own ends. –N

Guerrillas typically operate in small groups, and may be active in urban or rural regions, or both. Organisation is typically loose, with leadership by charismatic or effective individuals rather than a formal chain of command, although

a guerrilla force often has some of the trappings of a regular military. As guerrillas gain in power they tend to transition to a more conventional military organisation and style of operation.

Dealing with an insurgency can absorb large amounts of manpower and resources; indeed it may be in our interests for a war to be kept going rather than being won by the either side. If our opponents pull out of a region with burned fingers, that may suit our political ends and may present us with a propaganda opportunity, but having them bogged down in an interminable struggle may actually benefit us more. It also creates intelligence opportunities that might not otherwise exist; unstable regions are more 'porous' than a post-insurgency state is likely to be.

 Nations undergoing an active guerrilla war are even more unstable than nations engaged in more formal conflicts. This instability is a double-edged sword. One the one hand it is easier for us to operate, the borders are more porous, the local security forces have other issues to deal with, crime becomes commonplace, and the secretive movement of men and material becomes commonplace. However, all these advantages also work in favour of Our Other Enemy. –N

It is important to remember why we are involved in an insurgency. If we want a region cleared of foreign influences then that is our goal; if we prefer to leave it unstable and keep our opponents' attention focused on it then we must operate differently. The level and type of support furnished will be geared to preventing the defeat of the insurgents rather than facilitating their eventual victory – but we must ensure that they think we are working towards them winning their war. It may even be necessary to betray friendly insurgents to derail a potential victory – we may not be able to afford to be friends to the enemy of our enemy!

Guerrillas can cause a disproportionate amount of damage to our enemies (and to us if the situation is reversed) and can make the movement of even routine supply convoys a major operation involving heavy escorts and sweeps of the local area. In addition to ambushing supply runs and patrols, guerrillas might attack infrastructure such as bridges and canals, assassinate enemy officials and capture remote outposts.

Some actions will inevitably be taken purely for the sake of striking at the enemy, but co-belligerent guerrillas should be encouraged to make every action they take further their cause (actually, our cause!) either by obtaining arms, equipment and information or by denying something of value to the enemy. Operations should also be geared to maintaining and increasing popular support. This is vital to a successful guerrilla campaign as locals might be unwilling to fight but will provide support or harbour to the guerrillas.

Note that guerrilla groups are often close-knit and mistrustful even of other guerrillas fighting for the same cause. A campaign can be riddled with paranoia – often rightly so, since planting informers is a common way of finding and eliminating the guerrillas. As a result, a guerrilla force is typically highly compartmentalised, with groups varying in size, equipment, effectiveness and reputation.

This can be hazardous or useful depending on circumstance, but operatives must always remember that the guerrilla group they are associated with may not have the same outlook as others. Mistrust is natural, and hostility may not be for logical reasons. The enemy of our enemy is a co-belligerent, nothing more (see pg. 90 for more about working alongside such groups).

DETERMINING THE EFFECTIVENESS OF GUERILLA GROUPS

 As well as the use of Psychology to determine a group's motivations, as discussed in the *Dealing with Dissident Groups* box out on pg. 91, the investigators may wish to evaluate how effective a group will be in helping achieve the mission objective. This largely comes down to use of the Military Science skill, which will be similarly affected by organisational, language and cultural barriers.

The Keeper should add a penalty die to such rolls if the investigators do not speak the same language as the guerrillas, if they do not have adequate intelligence on the group or if the group does not have any defined leadership.

Thorough intelligence gathering about the group should afford a bonus die.

MISSIONS AND OPERATIONS

Although the terms are often used interchangeably, a mission tends to be small in either the number of personnel involved or the scope of its goals, whereas an operation tends to be larger and usually comprises multiple components; multiple assets and operatives may have missions to accomplish within the wider context of the operation. For example, operatives might be given a mission to obtain secret documents as part of a wider operation to find out what the opposition knows about our anti-ballistic missile defence systems.

There are some general rules for intelligence missions and operations, which apply whether operating with local guerrillas or carrying out a more normal intelligence operation. The first and most important rule is: no mission or operation should be carried out unless there is a worthwhile gain, and this must be balanced against risk.

It will almost always be more important to retain capability than to expend it for some single goal. A co-belligerent guerrilla unit wiped out on a badly planned mission deprives us of its use in the future and may create problems in our relationship with others, whilst the loss of our own operatives or their supporting assets is damaging to our cause in the long term.

Cancelling an operation once preparations are underway can be bad for morale and will upset local 'friendlies' who want to see action, but under most circumstances it is better to wait. It is rarely possible to attempt the same operation the same way twice, so avenues of approach should not be wasted. Note that local groups may not be reliable and may proceed anyway, either deliberately in defiance of our instructions or simply due to the vagaries of communication in the intelligence environment.

If an opportunity is unlikely to come again and the importance is great, then an operation might go ahead against rising odds. This is always expensive, however, in terms of personnel lost and the chance of utter failure. It must be remembered that any operation could be the last for any given intelligence network. Potential gain from the operation must be weighed against the possibility that our local intelligence network could be severely disrupted for some time to come, or even eliminated entirely.

MISSION AND OPERATIONAL PLANNING

Assuming that the operation or mission goes ahead, it will take place in several stages. The first, and probably the most important, is reconnaissance and information gathering. This applies equally to military and intelligence operations – we must know as much about the target and the likely response as possible. Political fallout must always be factored into operational planning, and may be a reason to abort the operation – our nation's political ends are always at the heart of any operation.

 Not quite always. There may be 'Other' considerations! -N

Subtlety and misdirection are our primary tools when carrying out an operation. Ideally, the target should not know something has happened until well after the operation is over, if at all. This is not always possible, so speed and stealth are also important considerations.

It is better to be ushered into the target location by a guard after presenting an invitation or to simply walk past dressed as a servant than to sneak by, but all of these are better than shooting your way in or trying to rush past the defences.

The 'louder' an operation becomes, the greater the risks and the more extreme the response. Political fallout is much greater from overt, 'loud' operations than polite, quiet ones. That said, if violence is to be used at all then it must be employed with ruthlessness and conviction. 'Force multipliers' must be brought to bear at the critical point; again these include speed, stealth, surprise and so forth.

These factors must be built into mission planning if they are to be employed usefully. The team assigned to obtain clothing and documents must be ready to hand them over to the team carrying out the mission, and operatives assigned to support withdrawal (such as drivers or couriers who are to be handed the 'take' from the mission) must be in place and ready to go. Information should be compartmentalised. For example, the facilitation team do not need to know what the main mission target is, and the entry team do not need to know the final destination for the 'take'. It is safest for everyone if information is shared on a need-to-know basis – but too little information can wreck a mission. Judging how much must be known by whom is a fine art and lies at the heart of good mission planning.

 You will have two missions to plan and execute, and the interweaving of them is crucial. Use your national cover's resources for insertion and extraction, and your best judgement on how to use such resources during the mission. Always keep in mind that we have few dedicated resources

other than our personnel, and all else should come from your mundane employer. -N

No two missions are exactly alike, and the same mission could require a different approach if repeated in a different locale or tactical situation. Often the approach used will be dictated by the opportunities that present themselves or the assets available. However, some common principles apply to almost all operations and missions.

Firstly, a large and complex operation – and usually even quite small and simple one – must be broken down into component parts. Sometimes these must be dispersed over time, which may be the only way to complete the task without blundering into an enemy ambush. 'Wait' is a valid operational order and personnel must be able to obey it. A single asset or operative who goes off half-cock can compromise a whole operation.

Tasks and information must be compartmentalised within a mission, and missions must be compartmentalised within an operation. An asset or an operative needs only to know what they are to do and how to go about it. They do not need to know if their actions are part of a wider operation or not. Indeed, it is better if they do not, under most circumstances.

Every mission is different, and often orders will be quite general. For example, an operative might be tasked with obtaining an unobtrusive delivery van and being at a certain place with it at a particular time. The details may not be important, other than the obvious consideration that the operative must not attract the attention of the authorities.

At times, orders will be quite specific. This is usually the case during a multi-part operation or a mission where the actions of various personnel must be coordinated. Such missions require far more detailed planning but may still include quite general components.

For example, a given operative might be instructed to pass critical documents to another at a certain time and place but allowed to use his own discretion as to how they obtain and transport them. It is often best when working with skilled personnel who know their environment to simply tell them what is required and what they must not do, and leave the details up to them.

MISSION COMPONENTS

Some missions will have all of the following components, others just a few:

Information Gathering can take place over a long period if necessary. Often this is part of routine operations and data that has already been obtained can be used, though some form of reconnaissance is usually necessary when planning an operation.

Early Facilitation is a matter of obtaining necessary items or ensuring that they can be quickly obtained when needed. Documents, clothing, vehicles and so forth can often be quietly assembled well before an operation without any danger of compromising it. It may be that an operation cannot even be contemplated without a particular item, circumstance or piece of information, so a large part of the early facilitation phase may be waiting for this to become available. Some items will be routinely available but there will usually be specific requirements. If possible, missions to obtain these will be separate from the overall operation, allowing it to be safely aborted if facilitation goes awry.

Timely Facilitation is carried out at the beginning of the operation, or sometimes once it is in motion. Any actions likely to cause alarm, such as stealing keys or vehicles, must be done as late as possible to limit the chance of detection. This can mean that some elements of a mission, such as

the vehicles to be used for extraction, are obtained after it has begun. Although this entails some risk, the chance of alerting the enemy must be weighed against the possibility that part of the operation could go awry.

Approach is usually the final opportunity to safely abort the mission. As operatives approach the target they may conduct their own appraisal of the situation or receive a final update from surveillance in place. A final abort/commit decision is made at this stage.

Infiltration of some form is required for most missions. This may be deceptive, covert (or, rarely) overt. The latter is only likely when carrying out a mission such as a violent snatch, an assassination that cannot be handled in some less obvious manner, or a rescue mission where there are no other good options. Infiltration ends when mission personnel reach their targets, but that does not translate to 'going loud'. Ideally the whole mission is carried out quietly and without the opposition being entirely sure what has happened.

Action is the critical phase of the mission, during which the operatives carry out their assigned task. There may be multiple actions within a mission – and certainly there will be within a large operation – and these may not all happen at the same time. Ideally this part of the mission is carried out 'on the quiet' and operatives will be able to avoid a 'grab and run' situation.

However, circumstances will dictate what is possible. Note that for some operatives, this phase consists of nothing more than watching and feeding information to others, or being in position to cover a withdrawal.

Exfiltration should ideally be carried out quietly and without fuss. If the aim is to extract personnel or critical documents, an exfiltration that involves rushing to waiting vehicles whilst a sniper provides covering fire is acceptable. However, a quiet exfiltration is best as it increases the chance of a clean operation (in other words, one that does not bring about a major response from the opposition).

Finalisation can sometimes be the beginning of a new mission. For example, once personnel have exfiltrated from their mission and passed stolen documents to a courier, the mission to bring them to the final recipient begins. For the personnel involved in a given mission, finalisation means ensuring that they are not followed or pursued, returning arms and equipment to wherever they are kept, and resuming normal activities. Finalisation requires as much planning as any other stage of an operation, and just as much care if the network is to remain viable in the long term.

All missions and operations are different, of course, and care must always be taken not to fall into habits or to simply follow doctrine when it is not appropriate. This can lead to an operation going awry or may give the opposition clear indication of the perpetrators.

Cleaning Up

All evidence as to the origin of personnel involved in a mission must be left behind. Personal effects are an obvious clue to the nationality and allegiance of an operative, and even items as simple as clothing labels can give away a great deal of information.

Weapons should be of 'international' origin; in other words, of a sort available on the open market, rather than being associated with a particular nation. The exception, of course, is when weaponry belonging to the opposition can be appropriated or when operating in an area flooded with arms of a particular origin.

Wherever possible, they should be sanitised. This means removing all serial numbers and other identifying marks that can allow a particular gun to be traced back to its origin.

It is, however, well known to all intelligence services that our operatives are sometimes supplied with a weapon that never had any serial numbers – which might be a giveaway in itself. It is better for a captured weapon to be examined and found to have been locally sanitised than to be obviously supplied to a covert operations force.

Tactical Considerations

Whether operating in the field or conducting an operation such as a kidnapping, tactical considerations are paramount. The difference between a five-second bag-and-grab with the target in a car and gone before any response materialises, and a shoot-out with the local police might be down to nothing more than good positioning and cooperation.

Operatives may sometimes have to work alone, or with only distant cover, but where possible a team should be deployed to maximise capability at the key point.

No more than one or two operatives can physically engage a given target without the risk of getting in one another's

way, so in cases of physical action such as kidnapping the usual set-up is for two operatives to overpower the target and others to facilitate the snatch. Additional personnel can prevent interference or clear the exfiltration route.

Mutual trust is vital; operatives must be able to concentrate on their own task without having to worry about a teammate's capabilities. It is not desirable to completely lose track of the overall situation but an operative whose task is to cover one approach should be able to do so without having to watch the others or struggle with a target who is trying to escape. The action should be sudden, made by surprise and over quickly. This is impossible when trying to carry out more than one task.

CLOSE PROTECTION DUTIES

Most comments that apply to infiltration, kidnap and assassination also apply to preventing them. An infiltration can be assisted by an observer who feeds information to the infiltrator or uses a suppressed rifle to prevent interference. Operatives protecting a building should consider likely spots for such support and be prepared to deal with them.

When protecting a VIP, common practice is to have one operative assigned as the bodyguard, who stays close to the principal, and other members of the close protection (CP) team dealing with potential threats as they emerge. Some members of the CP team may be a little distant from the principal, perhaps moving ahead to check alleys and side roads or lagging behind to prevent anyone moving up from behind.

An attack plan should always take into account that the target may have a scout out to the front or sides, so it may not be possible to simply hide and ambush them. There is also the possibility of some members of the CP team being outside the kill zone at the moment of a strike; it is not unknown for a kidnapping or assassination team to find itself taking fire from behind.

In the event of an attack, the bodyguard is responsible for last-ditch protection of the VIP, and for getting them to safety. The rest of the CP team are there to block the approach of potential hostiles and to engage them (physically or with firearms) where necessary. Again, mutual trust is important. In a good CP team the nearest operative deals with a potential problem whilst others watch their own sectors in case this is a distraction.

For example, if a shouting, agitated individual bursts out of a crowd and rushes towards the VIP, they will be stopped by the nearest member of the CP team. If this pulls them off station, others will move to maintain all-round cover and it is quite likely that everyone will glance is that direction as all-round awareness is vital in the close protection role.

However, the rest of the team should not become fixated on what is happening; they know it is being dealt with and they have their own sector to cover. Under most circumstances the threat will not reach the bodyguard, let alone the VIP.

A sloppy close protection team is easy to distract or draw off; a good one remains ready for anything even whilst dealing with a threat, and does not use disproportionate force to deal with a problem. Simple thugs might become distracted by beating up someone who got in the way or who seemed like a threat for a moment; skilled CP professionals do only what is necessary and then return to their mission, which is watching for new threats and ensuring the safety of their client.

Some VIPs use their 'minders' as muscle to show everyone how powerful and important they are, shoving people around and threatening them. However, high-end security tends to be polite, unobtrusive and vastly more effective. How hard it is to spot all the close protection operatives can be a useful measure of how good the security they provide will be.

COMBAT IN URBAN TERRAIN

Ideally, a mission will be accomplished without resorting to firearms, but as we do not live in an ideal world the most common environment an operative is likely to find themselves in a firefight is the built-up, urban environment. In such a cluttered environment, any exchange of fire is likely to be at close range. Use of cover, aggression and speed are often the decisive factors.

An operative cannot afford to become pinned down under cover. Missions are usually time-sensitive and opposition will increase over time. If forward progress is not possible then the only option is to break contact and withdraw; a protracted firefight will usually result in a failed mission whatever the outcome.

An operative may have no weapon larger than a handgun available, but more powerful armament should be provided if combat is expected. Shotguns and submachine guns are excellent for clearing a room or getting past a guard, and are 'handier' in tight spaces.

Urban combat is a three-dimensional business. Windows and rooftops can create firing points that negate cover, and shooters in these positions might not be spotted by someone whose attention is at ground level. If possible, it may be best to move through buildings rather than out in the open. Although this creates the possibility of an encounter at short range, this is more likely to be pre-empted by an alert operator than a rooftop sniper who might not be spotted before they open fire.

Whether on an individual or small-unit scale, any combat in urban terrain is likely to be a complex and chaotic affair. The enemy may have no idea how many hostiles they face or where they are, which can create advantages for a fast-moving and determined team.

The opposition will almost always have the advantage that they can defend their positions and wait for assistance; we must win, whereas they have only to avoid losing for long enough for help to arrive. If it does not seem likely that the operative can win quickly, combat should be avoided.

SELECTING SNIPER NESTS

Selecting a suitable sniper nest is similar to selecting a vantage point, as described on pg. 60. The only difference is that instead of a combined Stealth and Tradecraft roll, the sniper should make a combined Stealth and Firearms (Rifle/Shotgun) roll.

SMALL-UNIT MILITARY TACTICS

Whilst to a great extent open combat is the antithesis of intelligence operations, sometimes the best or only way to achieve a goal is through direct military action. This will usually take the form of a small unit of skilled personnel, heavily armed, making a sudden assault on an enemy position or possession, eliminating the defenders and then carrying out the mission at hand.

From the point of view of an intelligence operation, the first rule of combat is to leave it to the professionals. Wherever possible, if an operative is working with combat personnel then they should be allowed to handle their part of the task, with the operative hanging back until it is reasonably safe. This is more than simple self-preservation – the mission becomes meaningless without the operative.

It is worth noting that no combat zone is ever 100% safe, even after the shooting stops, so operatives need to be ready to defend themselves. However, unless an extra gun is critical to success the operative needs to stay out of the firing line as much as possible. That said, it may be useful to have a basic understanding of tactics.

AVOIDING COMBAT

If an investigator is working with a small military unit in pursuit of an objective, but wants to avoid being caught up in any combat, there are two main factors at play: luck and caution.

If the unit is operating in a combat zone, but is not setting out to engage the enemy, a group Luck roll will be required to avoid action. If this fails, the investigator will need to find cover.

A combined Stealth and Spot Hidden roll will allow an investigator to find and use a suitable hiding place, but this assumes that there is time to do so. If the unit encounters the enemy, refer to the *Striking the First Blow* (pg. 106) and *Diving for Cover* (pg. 113) sections of the *Call of Cthulhu* rulebook for guidance.

The individual infantryman, usually equipped with a semi-automatic or fully automatic rifle, is the basis of most combat teams. Specialists such as point men might carry shotguns or submachine guns, and submachine guns may be substituted for rifles if urban combat is expected.

However, for the most part combat takes the form of an exchange of rifle fire, supported by light automatic weapons. Most squads contain at least one light or general-purpose machine gun.

The basic principle is fire and movement; part of the force provides covering fire while another element moves to a better position. Once a good position is achieved – for example, one that allows enemy positions to be taken under a crossfire – the enemy can be eliminated or forced to withdraw from cover that no longer has any value.

Few firefights end with the total destruction of the opposing force, unless the enemy is cornered and refuses to surrender or is eliminated by grenades thrown into their final refuge. More commonly, one side retreats or flees leaving the other in possession of the battlefield.

For our purposes, terrain is virtually worthless, as are casualties inflicted upon the enemy. What matters is the ability to continue or complete the mission. Thus clearing an enemy force from the route is useful, as is taking possession of a signals station from which we might obtain useful intelligence. Winning a gunfight is a means to an end, nothing more.

INVESTIGATORS IN COMMAND

If one or more of the investigators is a covert operations specialist, the Keeper is advised to let them command the unit rather than following the orders of an NPC. Not every player has knowledge of military tactics, so the Keeper should be prepared to allow the investigator to make Military Science rolls in order to determine the best course of action.

DENIABILITY

There are times when overt action can be used to send a message, but this is a political matter and not usually one for the intelligence community. More commonly in our line of work we do not want anyone to know for sure that we were involved, even if they are aware that something has happened.

Deniability runs two ways; make sure that your actions against Our Other Enemy must be deniable to your mundane loyalties. The boss likes us to think of our agency jobs as

a cover, a cover you need to keep above all others.
– Rodriquez

The perfect outcome in many cases is that our actions go unnoticed, at least in the wider scheme of things. Failing that, if the opposition is unsure exactly what has happened and who is responsible then that is a good outcome. For example, if we can create a situation where a building has been destroyed by fire and both personnel and documents are missing, but the opposition does not know if they are dead, destroyed or taken, then this is a good outcome – especially if they do not know for sure which agency is responsible. Ideally, the enemy should not be able to say for definite that it was an operation at all.

It is inevitable that an operation might leave behind some evidence, in which case the only remaining recourse is deniability. That is to say, our political masters must be able to deny that they were involved with some degree of plausibility. The opposition must not be given clear proof that our agencies were responsible for a clear act.

Deniability can take the form of a plausible assertion or a polite fiction. The latter occurs when there is no certain proof but the opposition is pretty sure who is responsible. A 'polite fiction' that our political masters would never sanction such a thing might be acceptable because if the opposition admits that they know what we did and they are sure we did it, they have to act upon that or be seen to be weak. If they decide that it is not in their interest to act then they may choose to accept the polite fiction at face value.

The political game that we are involved in is complex and dangerous; a misstep could send us down the road to open warfare or a nuclear exchange. Above all else it is the duty of an operative to deny the opposition concrete information that could be used against us. This usually means taking care to clean up after an operation, to use sanitised weapons and to operate quietly and subtly. It can, however, mean desperate efforts to destroy equipment and documents as the opposition's personnel close in. It might also mean ensuring that personnel are not taken alive.

The fate of an operative who is captured can vary considerably. It is sometimes possible to effect a rescue or an exchange, and in some cases personnel have managed to avoid serious consequences and been released. This is rare, and only when the evidence against the operative is extremely slight.

 If Our Other Enemy captures you do not expect rescue. Take care of the issue yourself in a satisfactory and final manner. –N

PRISONER EXCHANGES

 If an investigator is captured in the course of a mission, whether they will be exchanged swiftly is largely determined by their value and whether their own government has a suitable prisoner to offer up in exchange. This can be resolved through a combined Trust and Luck roll. If this fails, the investigator's colleagues may try to convince their superiors in the intelligence services or government contacts to pursue the exchange on their behalf. Doing so could provide the basis for a short side-mission in a campaign, as the investigators negotiate the internal politics, bureaucracy and egos of their own intelligence services.

Damage caused by captured personnel can be minimised by compartmentalisation of information and by distancing planners with a knowledge of the network as a whole from hazardous operations. There is always some damage when personnel captured, and if the opposition are reasonably sure that they have an intelligence operative in custody then they may use very extreme means to obtain information. Operatives are trained to resist interrogation but there are limits to the endurance of any given person. Captors may never give up, or may torture operatives for the sake of revenge rather than any useful purpose.

It may be that death really is preferable to capture. If there are no other options, an operative may have to take the hard decision to terminate a colleague or ally who is in danger of impending capture, or to take their own life. With no prospects but suffering that ends only in betrayal of friends and country, death might be seen as a kindness.

In the final analysis, it is the duty of all operatives to keep secret information from the enemy and to deny them all assistance. A live operative might be used against their home country even if they do not give up any secrets, by causing political embarrassment or even escalation of the situation. In such circumstances, it may be the final duty of the operative to die rather than to aid the enemy. By preserving the deniability of our operations at the cost of their life, an operative may enable us to keep on opposing our enemies and prevent the escalation of a situation into a major international incident.

THE CONSEQUENCES OF FAILURE

The *World War Cthulhu: Cold War* rulebook provides guidance for Sanity and Trust awards and penalties following a mission, and our published scenarios include examples of such outcomes. Failed missions will probably prove quite detrimental to the careers and mental health of investigators, and this will only be compounded by their involvement with Section 46.

It is difficult enough to go through a debrief for a mission that resulted in the death of half your team without having to cover up the fact that they were devoured by a thousand-eyed monstrosity older than mankind.

I have seen the page, pages of me, me.

They are red, red, red and long, long, long. I have, have, to put them back, back. Get them off, off this bus stop floor.

They, they see me, they, they read, read me, me, me. – Stanton

CHAPTER SEVEN

APPENDICES: SPECIAL WEAPONS AND PRE-GENERATED CHARACTERS

APPENDIX A:
·SPECIAL WEAPONS·

A variety of special weapons are available to operatives working in the field. Some are issued by intelligence agencies and others can be obtained from the enemy. Note that much of this equipment is peculiar to a particular nation's armed forces or intelligence services and as such tends to make it rather obvious who sent a given operative.

The following weapons are either special purpose items or heavy weapons that are unlikely to be encountered outside of a war zone or a military base. They include underwater weapons, explosives, anti-tank systems and support weapons such as machine guns.

 Yeah, an Uzi might take down some small fry, but C4 or a Claymore certainly will. Too bad you won't get the chance to use one. It's not like you can file a request for monster hunting weapons. – Rodriguez

HANDGUNS

Welrod 'Silent Pistol'
Developed for use by SOE during World War Two, the Welrod pistol is not a combat weapon; it is an assassination tool. Chambered for 7.65mm (.32 ACP) ammunition it holds 8 rounds in the magazine, with a new round chambered manually by working the action. The grip must be dismantled to reload the magazine. The Welrod is virtually silent due to its internal suppressor.

Heckler & Koch P11
Introduced in 1976, the H&K P11 is an underwater pistol with five barrels, each capable of firing a single shot using electrical initiation. The entire barrel block must be replaced to reload the weapon.

SPP-1 Underwater Pistol
The Soviet SPP-1 is a four-barrel smoothbore pistol designed for use underwater. It is reloaded by replacing the block at the breech end of the barrels; this contains four rounds and effectively reloads each of the barrels. The SPP-1 has a double-action trigger and can be fired in or out of water, although it is much less accurate out of water than a conventional pistol.

LONGARMS

De Lisle Carbine
A World War Two-era weapon created using parts from a Lee-Enfield rifle and a Thompson submachine gun, the De Lisle has an integral suppressor that makes it almost completely silent. It uses a 7-round magazine and fires .45 ACP ammunition. It is effective out to about 250m, although accuracy drops beyond 100m.

HANDGUNS							
Weapon	Skill	Damage	Base Range	Attacks per round	Bullets in gun	HP's resistance	Malfunction
Welrod 'Silent Pistol'[1]	Firearms (Handgun)	1D8	5 yards	1	8	8	99
Heckler & Koch P11[2]	Firearms (Handgun)	1D8	15 yards/ 5 yards underwater	1 (3)	5	6	99
SPP-1 Underwater Pistol[2, 3]	Firearms (Handgun)	1D8	15 yards/ 5 yards underwater	1 (3)	4	6	99

[1] Due to the effective suppressor, any Listen rolls to detect the sound of a Welrod firing are made at an Extreme difficulty level.
[2] Can be used underwater, although doing so incurs a penalty die. Damage is halved when used underwater.
[3] Receives a penalty die when fired out of water.

APS Underwater Rifle

Introduced in 1975, the APS is a smoothbore rifle fed from a 26-round magazine. It is capable of automatic fire and will operate underwater or in air, though it is less accurate than a standard rifle and not well suited to general combat.

RPK

A variant of the AK-47 family of assault rifles, the RPK is basically an overgrown rifle with a longer, heavier barrel and a bipod. It can use AK assault rifle magazines or a larger 45-round magazine. A 70-round drum is also available, but is not widely used. The RPK is chambered for Soviet 7.62x39mm ammunition.

MACHINE GUNS

FN MAG 58/L7

The Belgian-made FN MAG machine gun is used by the armed forces of dozens of countries, most notably the United Kingdom, where it is designated L7. The MAG 58 is a true machine gun, with a quick-change barrel to allow one to cool while another continues to fire. It is fed from a belt composed of metal links, allowing a belt of any desired length to be produced. It is chambered for 7.62x51mm NATO ammunition. The MAG 58 is the classic general purpose machine gun and is often referred to as a GPMG (either spelled out or pronounced 'jimpy').

M60

The M60 machine gun is the standard support weapon of the US Army. It is chambered for 7.62x51mm NATO ammunition and fed from an ammunition belt. Early models required asbestos gloves for a barrel change, but later variants have the barrel attached to the carrying handle, which is used to hold the hot barrel as it is removed.

Maschinegewehr 3 (MG 3)

Developed from the World War Two-era MG 42, the MG 3 is chambered for 7.62x51mm NATO ammunition and has a very high rate of fire.

RPD/Type 56/Type 62

The Soviet-made RPD is a reliable and effective weapon, despite its somewhat crude appearance. Chambered for 7.62x39mm Soviet ammunition, it is fed from a 100-round belt housed in a drum. Versions of the same weapon are produced in China, where they are designated Type 56, and North Korea, where they are designated Type 62. RPD machine guns are widely exported and supplied to Soviet-backed insurgents worldwide.

LONGARMS							
Weapon	Skill	Damage	Base Range	Attacks per round	Bullets in gun	HP's resistance	Malfunction
De Lisle Carbine	Firearms (Rifle)	2D6+2	100 yards	2	7	15	00
APS Underwater Rifle[1]	Firearms (Rifle)	2D6	50 yards	1 or 2	26	8	99
RPK	Firearms (Rifle)	2D6+4	90 yards	1 (3) or Full Auto	30	10	99

[1] Can be used underwater, although doing so incurs a penalty die. Damage is halved when used underwater. Also receives a penalty die when shot on land.

RIFLES AND MACHINE GUNS

Weapon	Skill	Damage	Base Range	Attacks per round	Bullets in gun	HP's resistance	Malfunction
FN MAG 58/L7	Firearms (MG)	2D6+4	100 yards	Full Auto	50	12	99
M60	Firearms (MG)	2D6+4	110 yards	Full Auto	100	12	99
Maschinegewehr 3 (MG3)	Firearms (MG)	2D6+4	100 yards	Full Auto	50/100	12	99
RPD/Type 65/ Type 62	Firearms (MG)	2D6+4	110 yards	Full Auto	100	14	99
PKM	Firearms (MG)	2D6+4	110 yards	Full Auto	100	12	99

PKM

The PKM machine gun entered service in 1969 with Soviet and Warsaw Pact forces. It is a conventional general-purpose machine gun. 7.62x39mm Soviet ammunition is carried in a belt contained in a box, which stops the belt from swinging around and snagging on obstructions.

Rocket and Grenade Launchers

M2 Carl Gustav Recoilless Rifle

Developed in Sweden in the 1940s, the Carl Gustav is a reusable support weapon capable of firing an 84mm projectile out to a distance of a kilometre, although it is unlikely that most users could hit anything at even half that distance, especially if the target is moving. The Carl Gustav is used by the British Army, among others, providing a degree of anti-armour and anti-fortification capability.

RPG-7

The RPG-7 comprises a reusable launcher that is simple to use and extremely rigged, and a rocket-propelled grenade with a 70mm warhead. It is modestly effective against tanks and can easily destroy lighter vehicles. The RPG-7's maximum range is about 900m, but the effective range is much shorter. Most users are unlikely to score a hit at anything over 100-200m.

M72 LAW

A one-shot disposable rocket launcher capable of firing a 66mm warhead out to a distance of 200m, the M72 is reasonably effective against most tanks from the side but is unlikely to penetrate frontal armour. It is light enough to be carried by an infantry soldier until needed.

While it might be tempting to use a LAW or RPG to hunt big game, so to speak, these weapons present severe security issues. First and foremost, acquiring them. Even if you can manage to get one, 'off the books', so to speak, their use is hardly covert. - N

M79 Grenade Launcher

Also known as a 'bloop tube' for the noise it makes, or a 'thump gun', the M79 is the standard grenade launcher in use by the United States military. It fires a 40mm grenade that cannot be thrown. It is reloaded by break-open action, in the manner of many sporting shotguns. A skilled user can put a grenade through a window at 100-150 yards.

H&K 69A1 Grenatpistole

Developed as an under-barrel weapon to fit on an assault rifle, the 69A1 resembles a large pistol with an extendible shoulder stock. It functions as a standalone 40mm grenade launcher

M203 Grenade Launcher

The M203 is only just entering use at the beginning of the decade. It is designed to fit under the barrel of an M16 assault rifle, allowing one member of a squad to function as a grenadier without also depriving the squad of a rifleman. Like the M79, it can fire a wide range of grenades including high explosive anti-personnel rounds and a high explosive dual-purpose round designed to penetrate up to 5cm of light armour.

ROCKETS AND GRENADE LAUNCHERS

Weapon	Skill	Damage	Base Range	Attacks per round	Ammo Capacity	HP's resistance	Malfunction
M2 Carl Gustav Recoilless Rifle	Firearms (Heavy Weapons)	12D10/2 yards	500 yards	1	Separate	20	99
RPG-7	Firearms (Heavy Weapons)	3D10/2 yards	100 yards	1	1	14	99
M72 LAW	Firearms (Heavy Weapons)	8D10/1 yard	200 yards	1	1	14	99
M79 Grenade Launcher	Firearms (Heavy Weapons)	3D10/2 yards	100 yards	1	1	12	99
H&K 69A1 Grenatpistole	Firearms (Heavy Weapons)	3D10/2 yards	20 yards	1	1	12	99
M203 Grenade Launcher	Firearms (Heavy Weapons)	3D10/2 yards	20 yards	1	1	14	99

GRENADES

Fragmentation Grenades

The standard-issue US Army hand grenade, the M26, consists of an explosive core surrounded by notched wire, all housed within a metal casing. The grenade causes a certain amount of blast but its main killing power is due to fragments of wire and casing being hurled out at great speed. Lethal radius is about 15m. The M26 is due for replacement by the broadly similar M67 grenade in the 1970s. Fragmentation grenades in use by many other armed forces are generally similar in performance, such as the British L2A2.

Stun Grenades

Referred to as 'distraction' or 'stun' grenades, these weapons normally produce a bright flash or a very loud noise, or both. Flash grenades essentially overload the eye and cause blindness for a few seconds, whereas concussion-type grenades rely on the effect of overloading the ear to cause disorientation and deafness. There is a fire risk associated with these grenades, but they are not intended as incendiary weapons.

Gas and Smoke Grenades

Most gas grenades have a pyrotechnic and chemical reaction effect that produces a cloud of gas. Various agents generally known as tear gas are common, causing irritation to the eyes and, in cases of extreme inhalation, respiratory distress. Some gases are more likely to cause vomiting in addition to irritation. Other gases can be used, including the hallucinogenic BZ gas. Gas grenades are available in several forms, including rifle grenades, hand grenades, grenades launched from a specialist launcher and shotgun shells. Smoke is used by most military forces for concealment purposes, and various forms of coloured smoke grenades are also available for signalling purposes. Smoke is generated by pyrotechnic means, which can create a fire hazard.

Incendiary and Phosphorous Grenades

Incendiary grenades are designed to burn extremely hotly, destroying anything nearby and starting a fire. Most incendiary grenades use thermite and are referred to as thermite grenades, but may contain other substances as well. Incendiary grenades can be used to disable heavy equipment such as artillery weapons and will completely destroy smaller items. They are not very useful in a combat role, however.

Phosphorous grenades create an incendiary effect but will fling burning phosphorous out to a distance of several metres as well as creating a dense cloud of smoke. Phosphorous burns on contact with air and will cling to anything – and anyone – that it strikes, making it an excellent, if unpleasant, weapon.

GRENADES							
Weapon	Skill	Damage	Base Range	Attacks per round	Ammo Capacity	HP's resistance	Malfunction
Fragmentation Grenade	Throw	4D10/3 yards	STR/5 yards	1/2	1	10	99
Stun Grenade	Throw	1D10/3 yards[1]	STR/5 yards	1/2	1	10	99
Gas Grenade	Throw	N/A[2]	STR/5 yards	1/2	1	10	99
Smoke Grenade	Throw	N/A[3]	STR/5 yards	1/2	1	10	99
Incendiary Grenade	Throw	2D10[4]	STR/5 yards	1/2	1	10	99
Phosphorous Grenade	Throw	2D10/3 yards[4]	STR/5 yards	1/2	1	10	99

[1] All targets within 5 yards must pass a Hard CON roll or be blinded/deafened for 1D6 rounds.

[2] All targets within 5 yards or within the same enclosed space as a tear gas grenade must pass a Hard CON roll or be incapacitated by nausea and blindness for 1D6 rounds; failure also means that targets suffer a penalty die on all actions for the next 10 minutes.

Targets affected by BZ gas are not immediately incapacitated, but receive a penalty die on all actions until they next sleep. If the Keeper wishes to subject the investigator to hallucinations as a result of BZ gas, the **Delusions and Reality Checks** section on pg. 162 of *Call of Cthulhu* provides a useful framework. If the investigator is not suffering from a bout of madness, the Keeper may allow the investigator to use CON instead of Sanity to make Reality Checks, with no risk of Sanity loss for failed rolls. Investigators undergoing bouts of madness still risk losing SAN when making Reality Check rolls to see through drug-induced hallucinations.

[3] Smoke persists for 1D6 minutes, during which time any attempts to see in, out or through the smoke require a Hard Spot Hidden roll.

[4] An investigator using an incendiary or phosphorous grenade to start a fire must make a Luck roll to ensure that the fire catches and spreads.

RIOT GUNS

Federal Riot Gun

Although some shotguns are sometimes referred to as 'riot guns', this weapon is a less-lethal device that projects 'baton' rounds (large projectiles intended to knock down and stun opponents), tear gas, smoke and flare rounds. It can be encountered worldwide; various equivalent weapons also exist in other countries.

ARWEN

Becoming available in 1970, the Anti-Riot Weapon, Enfield (ARWEN) is a British 5-shot weapon fed from a rotary magazine. It can launch less-lethal baton rounds out to about 100m.

Schermuly Anti-Riot Gun

A British single-shot break-open weapon capable of firing a range of ammunition including baton and gas rounds, the Schermuly weapon and others like it are typical of the weapons in use when the media reports the use of 'rubber bullets' to control a situation.

NUCLEAR WARFARE

Nuclear weapons are an integral part of the Cold War, so it seems only fitting to include some information for the Keeper. The threat of nuclear annihilation is ever-present, and might be triggered by just one unexpected detonation. There are many possible plots involving nuclear weapons

RIOT GUNS

Weapon	Skill	Damage	Base Range	Attacks per round	Bullets in gun	HP's resistance	Malfunction
Federal Riot Gun	Firearms (Shotgun)	1D6[1]	20 yards	1	1	10	00
ARWEN	Firearms (Shotgun)	1D6[1]	20 yards	1	5	10	00
Schermuly Anti-Riot Gun	Firearms (Shotgun)	1D6[1]	20 yards	1	1	10	00

[1] Damage listed is given for baton rounds. As these are designed to incapacitate through pain, anyone hit with one should make a CON roll, even if the round does not inflict a Major Wound; failure means that the target is unable to take any action for the next 1D6 rounds.

All targets within 3 yards or within the same enclosed space as a detonating tear gas round must pass a Hard CON roll or be incapacitated by nausea and blindness for 1D6 rounds; failure also means that targets suffer a penalty die on all actions for the next 10 minutes.

The effect of smoke rounds persists for 1D6 minutes, during which time any attempts to see in, out or through the smoke require a Hard Spot Hidden roll.

that do not end in a mushroom cloud. Nuclear material to make bombs might have to be protected or denied someone who intends to use it, as might bomb-making components such as triggers.

Creating a nuclear weapon is actually quite difficult. Sufficient nuclear material must be obtained and contained in such a way that it remains below critical mass for nuclear fission but can quickly reach that mass when required. This typically means separating nuclear material within the bomb and creating a means to combine it hard and fast. If this is not done effectively the bomb's yield will be quite low – little better than a conventional bomb of the same size – though it will scatter toxic radioactive material, contaminating the local area.

It is possible to create a radiological dispersion device, or 'dirty bomb', using a conventional explosive device surrounded by nuclear material. A dirty bomb is not a nuclear weapon as such; its explosion is no bigger than a conventional bomb.

It can be considered the radioactive, toxic equivalent of a nail bomb; an anti-personnel weapon using some other material to enhance the effects of a conventional explosion. A device of this sort will not blast missile silos open, but it will kill a lot of people and make an area uninhabitable.

True nuclear weapons create a huge explosion that is rated in terms of kilotons or even megatons (thousands or millions of tons of TNT). A detonation causes several effects, starting with 'thermal bloom'. This is a pulse of infrared radiation that can incinerate nearby people and objects, and will cause fires at much greater distances. It is accompanied by radiation and an electromagnetic pulse which can destroy electronic devices in the area.

The blast effect is caused by air being pushed away from the explosion, and a secondary inrush of air as it comes back to fill the low-pressure area created. This causes the characteristic mushroom cloud as the air rises, taking with it dust and smoke particles.

A detonation at ground level causes a huge cloud of fallout, which can fall up to a hundred miles or more from the detonation site depending on the wind conditions. Radioactive fallout is highly dangerous by way of skin contact and ingestion or inhalation, but within 15-20 days most of its radioactivity will have decayed to safer levels.

A nuclear device can also be exploded above the target, creating a downward shock effect intended to crack hard targets such as missile silos or bunkers. Lighter structures will be affected by the blast as it radiates out from the detonation. There will usually be a zone of total annihilation

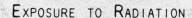

Exposure to Radiation

Radiation should be treated in the same manner as poisons. The Keeper should have investigators make a CON roll when first exposed, and then at the frequency listed in the guidelines below. Success means the investigator does not suffer the effects for the period of exposure. If the investigator fails the roll, use the following guidelines to determine the effect of exposure:

MILD EXPOSURE: Low-level fallout. Internal exposure to a tiny quantity of mildly radioactive material, such as radium.

CON roll every month. Failure results in 1D10 damage and 1D10 loss of APP from burns and hair loss. If they survive, afterwards the investigator must pass a Luck roll with two bonus dice to avoid developing cancer, organ failure, blindness or another chronic, life-threatening health problem.

MODERATE EXPOSURE: Significant fallout. Exposure to low concentrations of radioactive gas. Internal exposure to small quantity of radioactive material (effects will continue until subject dies).

CON roll every day. Failure results in 1D10 damage and 1D10 loss of APP from burns and hair loss. If they survive, afterwards the investigator must pass a Luck roll with one bonus die to avoid developing cancer, organ failure, blindness or another chronic, life-threatening health problem.

STRONG EXPOSURE: Exposure to a the site of a recent nuclear weapon detonation. Exposure to strong concentrations of radioactive gas. Internal exposure to larger quantity of radioactive material (if swallowed, effects will continue until subject dies).

CON roll every hour. Failure results in 1D10 damage and 1D10 loss of APP from burns and hair loss. If they survive, afterwards the investigator must pass a Luck roll to avoid developing cancer , organ failure, blindness or another chronic or life-threatening health problem.

Intense exposure: Direct exposure to a nuclear core.

CON roll every round. Failure results in 1D10 damage and 1D10 loss of APP from burns and hair loss. If they survive, afterwards the investigator must pass a Hard Luck roll to avoid developing cancer, organ failure, blindness or another chronic, life-threatening health problem.

surrounded by a region of decreasing damage characterised by fires and blast effects.

Nuclear devices range from 'suitcase nukes' (demolition charges that can be carried in a light vehicle) through tactical weapons such as missiles, nuclear depth charges and the like, right up to multi-megaton warheads intended to destroy cities or missile silos. Most weapons use nuclear fission, but more powerful weapons can be produced using nuclear fusion. These thermonuclear weapons are harder to produce and are beyond the means of all but the most advanced nations.

Enhanced radiation weapons ('neutron bombs') are a specialist version of a standard nuclear weapon intended to create a greater radiation pulse. They still have blast and heat effect, but produce more direct radiation with the effect that they will kill personnel at a greater distance by radiation effects without increasing damage to infrastructure.

M28/M29 Davy Crockett

Nuclear weapons come in many shapes and sizes, from large strategic missile warheads and bombs designed to be delivered by aircraft through 'battlefield' or tactical nuclear missiles. There is even an infantry-portable 'nuclear bazooka'. This is the M28/M29 Davy Crockett nuclear weapon, which can be fired from a tripod out to a distance of 1.5-2.5 miles. Its blast and radiation burst would almost certainly kill everyone within a quarter-mile.

The Davy Crockett weapon is currently in use with the US Army, though it has been phased out of European deployment in the past few years. There were those who opposed its withdrawal, citing weapons of this sort as the only way to stop the 'Red Steamroller', whose assault seems inevitable.

 This weapon stands as an indicator of the times in which our operatives live, and the reason why they must succeed in their missions. A world that feels the need for weapons of this sort stands on a knife-edge even without the intervention of Our Other Enemy. – N

PERCIVAL ST JOHN

NATIONALITY : British
AGE : 57
SEX : Male
PERSONALITY : Leader

PERSONAL DESCRIPTION

Portly, jowled and hook-nosed, St John has wispy white hair surrounding his bald crown. His avuncular manner is carefully practiced, and he enjoys playing the role of the harmless old duffer. While his tastes are somewhat eccentric, St John is always perfectly turned out, favouring light-coloured suits and cravats.

BACKGROUND

A relic of wartime intelligence and an original member of Network N, St John returned to SIS after the dissolution of SOE in 1946. He has worked a variety of foreign postings, specialising in counter-intelligence. His cold-blooded ability to distance himself from the human cost of his actions makes him exceptionally good at his job, if a dangerous person to work with.

IDEOLOGY/BELIEFS

Espionage is best considered as a game. It is arrogance to consider oneself a player: most of us are sacrificial pawns at best.

TRAITS

St John is obsessed with small details, and often absent-mindedly corrects the grammar of those around him.

INITIAL MYTHOS EXPERIENCE

As a young teenager, St John and his brother Richard used to explore the ruins of the recently demolished Exham Priory. The house's reputation for evil secrets made it irresistible to two thrill-seeking adolescents. Despite the thorough destruction of the house itself, the brothers found cracks and crevices amidst the rubble. After a bit of planning, they made their way down into the darkness using ropes and lanterns, and discovered what seemed like an entire hidden world there. They also discovered that they were not alone, that misshapen things that resembled men only in the worst possible ways dwelt in the darkness, devouring anything they could catch. St John barely escaped, and his nightmares are filled with the screams of his brother as he was snatched down into the darkness. Richard was never seen again.

INVESTIGATOR

NAME	Percival St John
PLAYER		PERSONALITY	Leader
OCCUPATION	Intelligence Officer
SPECIALISM	Field Officer
AGE	57	SEX	Male
NATIONALITY	British	AGENCY	SIS

CHARACTERISTICS

STR	50 / 25 / 10	DEX	40 / 20 / 8	INT IDEA	80 / 40 / 16
CON	50 / 25 / 10	APP	50 / 25 / 10	POW	70 / 35 / 14
SIZ	60 / 30 / 12	EDU	60 / 30 / 12	MOVE RATE	5

HIT POINTS

| MAX HP | 11 | | TEMP. INSANE | | START |

| MAJOR WOUND | | INDEF. INSANE | | MAX |

Dying 0 1 2
Unconscious 3 4 5
6 7 8 9 10
(11) 12 13 14 15
16 17 18 19 20

SANITY

Insane 0 1 2 3 4 5 6 7 8 9 10 11 12 13 14
15 16 17 18 19 20 21 22 23 24 25 26 27 28 29 30 31
32 33 34 35 36 37 38 39 40 41 42 43 44 45 46 47 48
49 50 51 52 53 54 55 56 57 58 59 60 61 62 63 64 65
66 (67) 68 69 70 71 72 73 74 75 76 77 78 79 80 81 82
83 84 85 86 87 88 89 90 91 92 93 94 95 96 97 98 99

LUCK

Out of Luck 1 2 3 4 5 6 7 8 9 10 11 12 13 14 15
16 17 18 19 20 21 22 23 24 25 26 27 28 29 30 31 32 33 34 35 36
37 38 39 40 41 42 43 44 45 46 47 48 49 50 51 52 53 54 55 56 57
58 59 60 61 62 63 64 65 66 67 68 69 (70) 71 72 73 74 75 76 77 78
79 80 81 82 83 84 85 86 87 88 89 90 91 92 93 94 95 96 97 98 99

| MAX MP | 14 |

MAGIC POINTS

0 1 2 3 4
5 6 7 8 9
10 11 12 13 (14)
15 16 17 18 19
20 21 22 23 24

INVESTIGATOR SKILLS

Skill	%	
☐ Accounting (10%)		
✦ Anthropology (01%)	21%	10 / 4
☐ Appraise (05%)		
☐ Archaeology (01%)		
☐ Art/Craft (05%)		
☐		
☐		
☐ Art/Craft (Forgery) (05%)		
☐ Artillery (01%)		
✦ Charm (15%)	50%	25 / 10
☐ Climb (20%)		
☐ Computer Use (05%)		
✦ Credit Rating (00%)	60%	30 / 12
☐ Cryptography (00%)		
✦ Cthulhu Mythos (00%)	1%	1 / 1
✦ Demolitions (00%)	20%	10 / 4
☐ Disguise (05%)		

Skill	%	
✦ Dodge (Half DEX)	20%	10 / 4
✦ Drive Auto (20%)	40%	20 / 8
☐ Electrical Repair (10%)		
☐ Electronics (01%)		
✦ Fast Talk (05%)	50%	25 / 10
✦ Fighting (Brawl) (25%)	40%	20 / 8
☐		
☐ Firearms (Handgun (20%)		
☐ Firearms (Rifle/ Shotgun) (25%)		
☐		
☐		
☐ First Aid (30%)		
✦ History (20%)	40%	20 / 8
☐ Intimidate (15%)		
☐ Jump (20%)		
✦ Language (German)	60%	30 / 12
✦ Language (Russian)	50%	25 / 10

Skill	%	
☐ Language (Own) (EDU)		
✦ Law (05%)	40%	20 / 8
☐ Library Use (20%)		
☐ Listen (20%)		
☐ Locksmith (01%)		
☐		
☐ Mechanical Repair (10%)		
☐ Medicine (01%)		
☐ Military Science (00%)		
☐ Natural World (10%)		
☐ Navigate (10%)		
✦ Occult (05%)	25%	12 / 5
☐ Operate Heavy Machinery (01%)		
☐ Organisation Knowledge (01%)		
✦ Organisation Knowledge (Soviet Union)	60%	30 / 12
✦ Organisation Knowledge (Eastern Europe)	50%	25 / 10
✦ Persuade (10%)	70%	35 / 14

Skill	%	
✦ Pilot (01%)	21%	10 / 4
☐		
☐ Psychoanalysis (01%)		
✦ Psychology (10%)	80%	40 / 16
☐ Ride (05%)		
☐ Science (01%)		
☐		
✦ Signals (01%)	21%	10 / 4
☐ Sleight of Hand (10%)		
✦ Spot Hidden (25%)	50%	25 / 10
☐ Stealth (20%)		
☐ Survival (10%)		
☐		
☐ Swim (20%)		
☐ Throw (20%)		
☐ Track (10%)		
✦ Tradecraft (01%)	70%	35 / 14

WEAPONS

Weapon	Regular	Hard	Extreme	Damage	Range	Attacks	Ammo	Malf
Unarmed	40	20	8	1d3+db	-	1	-	-
Webley MK IV revolver				1d10				

COMBAT

DAMAGE BONUS	None
BUILD	0
DODGE	20

BACKSTORY

PERSONAL DESCRIPTION Portly, jowled and hook-nosed, St John has wispy white hair surrounding his bald crown. His avuncular manner is carefully practiced, and he enjoys playing the role of the harmless old duffer. While his tastes are somewhat eccentric, St John is always perfectly turned out, favouring light-coloured suits and cravats.

WHY ARE YOU A SPY? Ego. St John sees espionage as a game and himself as a grandmaster.

SIGNIFICANT PEOPLE Michael Brownlow, a new officer in the section who St John has found himself mentoring. The boy is still green, but cunning, and reminds St John of himself when he was young.

MEANINGFUL LOCATIONS The Greene Club in St James's, where St John meets colleagues from Section 46 for a sauna every Sunday morning.

TREASURED POSSESSIONS A poison capsule St John took from an SS officer in the war. It may come in useful one day.

TRAITS St John is obsessed with small details, and often absent-mindedly corrects the grammar of those around him.

INJURIES AND SCARS

PHOBIAS AND MANIAS

ARCANE TOMES, SPELLS AND ARTEFACTS

ENCOUNTERS WITH STRANGE ENTITIES When they were children, St John and his brother, Richard, explored the ruins of the notorious Exham Priory. Richard was taken into the darkness by a misshapen humanoid creature and never seen again.

GEAR AND POSSESSIONS

Bentley T series four-door saloon

CASH AND ASSETS

SPENDING LEVEL £100
STANDARD OF LIVING Wealthy
CASH £ 600 / P
ASSETS £60,000

1 POUND (£) = 100 PENCE (P)

TRUST

AGENCY	%
SIS	40% (20/8)
Section 46	40% (20/8)

FELLOW INVESTIGATORS

Character:
Player:

Character:
Player:

Character:
Player:

Character:
Player:

ME

Character:
Player:

Character:
Player:

Character:
Player:

JOZSEF LANTOS/JOSEPH DOWNS

NATIONALITY : Hungarian
AGE : 28
SEX : Male
PERSONALITY : Thinker

PERSONAL DESCRIPTION

Tall, dark-haired and with sharp, intelligent eyes, Lantos is a handsome man and uses this to his advantage. He is also a natural mimic, and while his Hungarian accent is noticeable when he is not trying to disguise it, he affects a perfect English accent most of the time.

BACKGROUND

The younger brother of one of the student leaders of the demonstrations that sparked the 1956 uprising in Hungary. Lantos was smuggled out of Hungary by Clarence Downs, an SIS agent who had been working with Lantos' brother, after the rest of his family were killed by the Soviets. Downs adopted Lantos and raised him in England, but Lantos never forgets where he came from. His background, language skills and facility for deception made him a natural recruit for SIS, and he has been working as an agent since leaving university.

IDEOLOGY/BELIEFS

The Soviets are responsible for the deaths of too many people Lantos has loved, and they need to pay.

TRAITS

Speaks thoughtfully and carefully, leaving long silences while he considers what to say next.

INITIAL MYTHOS EXPERIENCE

Disobeying direct orders, Lantos broke into an address in West Berlin that a contact had told him was a Stasi safe house. Instead of finding the Hungarian double agent he had been tracking, Lantos found himself facing an old man living in skin-crawling filth. The man had a strangely elongated face and his mouth opened far too wide as he cried out in alarm. As the man stumbled towards Lantos, reaching out with sharp and filthy fingernails, Lantos panicked and shot him. The man fell back and slowly dissolved into a pool of foul liquid that writhed with small, worm-like shapes. Lantos never reported the experience to his superiors, but the short period of psychiatric care he required brought him to the attention of N's associates.

INVESTIGATOR

NAME József Lantos/Joseph Downs

PLAYER _____ **PERSONALITY** Thinker

OCCUPATION Intelligence Officer

SPECIALISM Field Officer

AGE 28 **SEX** Male

NATIONALITY Hungarian **AGENCY** SIS

CHARACTERISTICS

STR	60	30 / 12	**DEX**	80	40 / 16	**INT IDEA**	60	30 / 12
CON	50	25 / 10	**APP**	70	35 / 14	**POW**	50	25 / 10
SIZ	50	25 / 10	**EDU**	40	20 / 8	**MOVE RATE**	9	

HIT POINTS

Dying	0	1	2
Unconscious	3	4	5
6	7	8	9	10
(11)	12	13	14	15
16	17	18	19	20

MAX HP 11

TEMP. INSANE

START

MAJOR WOUND

INDEF. INSANE

MAX

SANITY

Insane 0 1 2 3 4 5 6 7 8 9 10 11 12 13 14
15 16 17 18 19 20 21 22 23 24 25 26 27 28 29 30 31
32 33 34 35 36 37 38 39 40 41 42 43 44 45 46 47 (48)
49 50 51 52 53 54 55 56 57 58 59 60 61 62 63 64 65
66 67 68 69 70 71 72 73 74 75 76 77 78 79 80 81 82
83 84 85 86 87 88 89 90 91 92 93 94 95 96 97 98 99

LUCK

Out of Luck 1 2 3 4 5 6 7 8 9 10 11 12 13 14 15
16 17 18 19 20 21 22 23 24 25 26 27 28 29 30 31 32 33 34 35 36
37 38 39 40 41 42 43 44 45 46 47 48 49 (50) 51 52 53 54 55 56 57
58 59 60 61 62 63 64 65 66 67 68 69 70 71 72 73 74 75 76 77 78
79 80 81 82 83 84 85 86 87 88 89 90 91 92 93 94 95 96 97 98 99

MAX MP 10

MAGIC POINTS

0 1 2 3 4
5 6 7 8 9
(10) 11 12 13 14
15 16 17 18 19
20 21 22 23 24

INVESTIGATOR SKILLS

☐ Accounting (10%)			
☐ Anthropology (01%)			
☐ Appraise (05%)			
☐ Archaeology (01%)			
☐ Art/Craft (05%)			
☐			
☐			
☐ Art/Craft (Forgery) (05%)			
☐ Artillery (01%)			
☑ Charm (15%)	60%	30 / 12	
☐ Climb (20%)			
☐ Computer Use (05%)			
☑ Credit Rating (00%)	40%	20 / 8	
☐ Cryptography (00%)			
☑ Cthulhu Mythos (00%)	1%	1 / 1	
☐ Demolitions (00%)			
☑ Disguise (05%)	60%	30 / 12	

☑ Dodge (Half DEX)	60%	30 / 12	
☑ Drive Auto (20%)	50%	25 / 10	
☑ Electrical Repair (10%)	30%	15 / 6	
☐ Electronics (01%)			
☑ Fast Talk (05%)	70%	35 / 14	
☑ Fighting (Brawl) (25%)	60%	30 / 12	
☐			
☐ Firearms (Handgun) (20%)			
☐ Firearms (Rifle/Shotgun) (25%)			
☐			
☐			
☑ First Aid (30%)	50%	25 / 10	
☐ History (20%)			
☐ Intimidate (15%)			
☐ Jump (20%)			
☑ Language (English)	60%	30 / 12	
☑ Language (Russian)	21%	10 / 4	

☐ Language (Own) (EDU)			
☑ Law (05%)	50%	25 / 10	
☐ Library Use (20%)			
☐ Listen (20%)			
☑ Locksmith (01%)	21%	10 / 4	
☐			
☑ Mechanical Repair (10%)	30%	15 / 6	
☐ Medicine (01%)			
☐ Military Science (00%)			
☐ Natural World (10%)			
☑ Navigate (10%)	40%	20 / 8	
☐ Occult (05%)			
☐ Operate Heavy Machinery (01%)			
☐ Organisation Knowledge (01%)			
☑ Organisation Knowledge (Soviet Union)	40%	20 / 8	
☑ Organisation Knowledge (Eastern Europe)	60%	30 / 12	
☐ Persuade (10%)			

☐ Pilot (01%)			
☐			
☐ Psychoanalysis (01%)			
☑ Psychology (10%)	50%	25 / 10	
☐ Ride (05%)			
☐ Science (01%)			
☐			
☑ Signals (01%)	21%	10 / 4	
☐ Sleight of Hand (10%)			
☑ Spot Hidden (25%)	80%	40 / 16	
☐ Stealth (20%)			
☐ Survival (10%)			
☐			
☐ Swim (20%)			
☐ Throw (20%)			
☐ Track (10%)			
☑ Tradecraft (01%)	70%	35 / 14	

WEAPONS

Weapon	Regular	Hard	Extreme	Damage	Range	Attacks	Ammo	Malf
Unarmed	60	30	12	1d3+db	-	1	-	-
Switchblade				1d4				

COMBAT

DAMAGE BONUS	None
BUILD	0
DODGE	60

BACKSTORY

PERSONAL DESCRIPTION _Tall, dark-haired and with sharp, intelligent eyes, Lantos is a handsome man and uses this to his advantage. He is also a natural mimic, and while he his Hungarian accent is noticeable when he is not trying to disguise it, he affects a perfect English accent most of the time._

WHY ARE YOU A SPY? _Ideology. The Soviets are responsible for the deaths of too many people Lantos has loved, and they need to pay._

SIGNIFICANT PEOPLE _Lantos's adoptive father, Clarence Downs, an SIS officer who smuggled Lantos out of Hungary during the failed revolution in 1956, following the death of his family._

MEANINGFUL LOCATIONS _The Golden Lion in Soho, a gay bar where Lantos spends the occasional evening when he is sure no one from the security service is watching him._

TREASURED POSSESSIONS _His brother's watch, the only memento Lantos has of his family._

TRAITS _Speaks thoughtfully and carefully, leaving long silences while he considers what to say next._

INJURIES AND SCARS

PHOBIAS AND MANIAS

ARCANE TOMES, SPELLS AND ARTEFACTS

ENCOUNTERS WITH STRANGE ENTITIES _While searching a Stasi safe house in West Berlin, Lantos encountered a grubby old man with strangely elongated features, who had apparently broken in. The man attacked Lantos, who panicked and stabbed his assailant. The man dissolved into a pool of foul liquid that writhed with worms._

GEAR AND POSSESSIONS

Gold cigarette lighter
A good selection of stylish suits

CASH AND ASSETS

SPENDING LEVEL _£20_
STANDARD OF LIVING _Average_
CASH £ _160_ / P
ASSETS _£4,000_

1 POUND (£) = 100 PENCE (P)

TRUST

AGENCY	%
SIS	40% (20/8)
Section 46	40% (20/8)

FELLOW INVESTIGATORS

Character:
Player:

Character:
Player:

Character:
Player:

Character:
Player:

ME

Character:
Player:

Character:
Player:

Character:
Player:

Character:
Player:

LAURA SHELDEN

NATIONALITY : British
AGE : 34
SEX : Female
PERSONALITY : Bruiser

PERSONAL DESCRIPTION

Small, with a wiry build that hides how muscular she is. Blonde hair, usually tied back in a ponytail. High cheekbones, pale skin and dead eyes. Shelden rarely speaks unless spoken to.

BACKGROUND

Shelden was born in Malay, the daughter of a British rubber plantation owner. The Malayan National Liberation Army stormed the plantation in 1948, killing her father and taking Shelden as a hostage. Some months later she was found in the jungle by the British Army, skinny, dressed in rags and carrying a bloody machete. She rarely talks about what happened to her, but the notes made by an Army medic at the time suggest that she had killed one of her captors in his sleep and escaped. She had been hiding in the jungle for months. Shelden was just 10 years old. Shelden grew into a troubled teenager, involved in a string of violent incidents that kept her in borstal. After N read her file and pulled some strings, Shelden was recruited into SIS as a young adult. When Shelden is assigned to a mission, unpleasantness is usually expected.

IDEOLOGY/BELIEFS

Survival is all that matters, no matter the cost.

TRAITS

Sits extremely still unless she is actively doing something.

INITIAL MYTHOS EXPERIENCE

When Shelden hid in the jungle as a child, she took shelter in a crumbling old stone building, overgrown with creepers and covering the entrance to a network of caves. There she met things that lived in the dark, things that were almost like men but with very different appetites. They sheltered her until her eventual rescue, although Shelden doesn't know whether they saw her as their ward or a future meal. The psychiatrist that N makes Shelden see has helped her realise that her fears are less about what happened to her in the dark and more about what she did there. Shelden finds it difficult to stomach meat to this day.

WORLD WAR CTHULHU — COLD WAR

INVESTIGATOR

NAME: Laura Shelden
PLAYER: _____
PERSONALITY: Bruiser
OCCUPATION: Intelligence Officer
SPECIALISM: Covert Actions Operative
AGE: 34
SEX: Female
NATIONALITY: British
AGENCY: SIS

CHARACTERISTICS

STR	70	35 / 14	DEX	80	40 / 16	INT IDEA	50	25 / 10
CON	60	30 / 12	APP	50	25 / 10	POW	50	25 / 10
SIZ	60	30 / 12	EDU	40	20 / 8	MOVE RATE	9	

HIT POINTS

MAX HP: 12
TEMP. INSANE
START
MAJOR WOUND
INDEF. INSANE
MAX

Dying 0 1 2
Unconscious 3 4 5
6 7 8 9 10
11 (12) 13 14 15
16 17 18 19 20

SANITY

Insane 0 1 2 3 4 5 6 7 8 9 10 11 12 13 14
15 16 17 18 19 20 21 22 23 24 25 26 27 28 29 30 31
32 33 34 35 36 37 38 39 40 41 42 43 44 45 (46) 47 48
49 50 51 52 53 54 55 56 57 58 59 60 61 62 63 64 65
66 67 68 69 70 71 72 73 74 75 76 77 78 79 80 81 82
83 84 85 86 87 88 89 90 91 92 93 94 95 96 97 98 99

LUCK

Out of Luck 1 2 3 4 5 6 7 8 9 10 11 12 13 14 15
16 17 18 19 20 21 22 23 24 25 26 27 28 29 30 31 32 33 34 35 36
37 38 39 40 41 42 43 44 45 46 47 48 49 50 51 52 53 54 55 56 57
58 59 (60) 61 62 63 64 65 66 67 68 69 70 71 72 73 74 75 76 77 78
79 80 81 82 83 84 85 86 87 88 89 90 91 92 93 94 95 96 97 98 99

MAGIC POINTS

MAX MP: 10

0 1 2 3 4
5 6 7 8 9
(10) 11 12 13 14
15 16 17 18 19
20 21 22 23 24

INVESTIGATOR SKILLS

Skill	%	
☐ Accounting (10%)		
☐ Anthropology (01%)		
☐ Appraise (05%)		
☐ Archaeology (01%)		
☐ Art/Craft (05%)		
☐		
☐		
☐ Art/Craft (Forgery) (05%)		
☐ Artillery (01%)		
☐ Charm (15%)		
☑ Climb (20%)	50%	25 / 10
☐ Computer Use (05%)		
☑ Credit Rating (00%)	40%	20 / 8
☐ Cryptography (00%)		
☑ Cthulhu Mythos (00%)	3%	1 / 1
☑ Demolitions (00%)	50%	25 / 10
☐ Disguise (05%)		

Skill	%	
☑ Dodge (Half DEX)	60%	30 / 12
☑ Drive Auto (20%)	40%	20 / 8
☐ Electrical Repair (10%)		
☐ Electronics (01%)		
☐ Fast Talk (05%)		
☑ Fighting (Brawl) (25%)	80%	40 / 16
☐		
☑ Firearms (Handgun (20%)	70%	35 / 14
☐ Firearms (Rifle/Shotgun) (25%)		
☐		
☐		
☑ First Aid (30%)	50%	25 / 10
☐ History (20%)		
☑ Intimidate (15%)	60%	30 / 12
☑ Jump (20%)	50%	25 / 10
☑ Language (Malay)	40%	20 / 8
☐		

Skill	%	
☐ Language (Own) (EDU)		
☐ Law (05%)		
☐ Library Use (20%)		
☐ Listen (20%)		
☑ Locksmith (01%)	21%	10 / 4
☐		
☐ Mechanical Repair (10%)		
☐ Medicine (01%)		
☐ Military Science (00%)		
☐ Natural World (10%)		
☐ Navigate (10%)		
☐ Occult (05%)		
☐ Operate Heavy Machinery (01%)		
☐ Organisation Knowledge (01%)		
☑ Organisation Knowledge (Southeast Asia)	50%	25 / 10
☐		
☐ Persuade (10%)		

Skill	%	
☐ Pilot (01%)		
☐		
☐ Psychoanalysis (01%)		
☑ Psychology (10%)	30%	15 / 6
☐ Ride (05%)		
☐ Science (01%)		
☐		
☐ Signals (01%)		
☐ Sleight of Hand (10%)		
☑ Spot Hidden (25%)	60%	30 / 12
☑ Stealth (20%)	70%	35 / 14
☑ Survival (10%) (Jungle)	30%	15 / 6
☐		
☑ Swim (20%)	40%	20 / 8
☐ Throw (20%)		
☐ Track (10%)		
☐ Tradecraft (01%)		

WEAPONS

Weapon	Regular	Hard	Extreme	Damage	Range	Attacks	Ammo	Malf
Unarmed	80	40	16	1d3+db	-	1	-	-
Commando Knife				1d8 + db				
Walther PPK .32 pistol				1d8				

COMBAT

DAMAGE BONUS: +1d4
BUILD: +1
DODGE: 60

BACKSTORY

PERSONAL DESCRIPTION _Average height, with a wiry build that hides how muscular she is. Blonde hair, usually tied back in a ponytail. High cheekbones, pale skin and dead eyes. Shelden rarely speaks unless spoken to._

WHY ARE YOU A SPY? _Shelden was recruited into SIS at N's behest. He saw her emotionless manner, propensity for violence and experience of the Mythos as assets._

SIGNIFICANT PEOPLE _Billy, a tramp who sleeps rough in Tower Hamlets Cemetery Park. There is something about him that reminds Shelden of her childhood, and she is drawn to him._

MEANINGFUL LOCATIONS _Tower Hamlets Cemetery Park. Shelden goes for long, peaceful walks amongst the wild undergrowth, crumbling gravestones and collapsed tombs._

TREASURED POSSESSIONS _A small soapstone carving that Shelden has had since she was a child. It resembles a man, but with canine features. She talks to it in her dreams._

TRAITS _Sits extremely still unless she is actively doing something._

INJURIES AND SCARS _An old, deep scar over her right eye._

PHOBIAS AND MANIAS

ARCANE TOMES, SPELLS AND ARTEFACTS

ENCOUNTERS WITH STRANGE ENTITIES _As a child in Malay, Shelden took shelter from guerillas in an ancient, crumbling building. There she was watched over by creatures that resembled humans, but had strange, unwholesome appetites. They sheltered her until her eventual rescue, although Shelden doesn't know whether they saw her as their ward or a future meal._

GEAR AND POSSESSIONS

Mini Cooper
Antique Fairbairn-Sykes fighting knife

CASH AND ASSETS

SPENDING LEVEL _£20_
STANDARD OF LIVING _Average_
CASH £ _160_ / **P**
ASSETS _£4,000_

1 POUND (£) = 100 PENCE (P)

TRUST

AGENCY	%
SIS	30% (20/8)
Section 46	50% (20/8)

FELLOW INVESTIGATORS

Character:
Player:

Character:
Player:

Character:
Player:

ME

Character:
Player:

Character:
Player:

Character:
Player:

ELEANOR GYSBERS

NATIONALITY: American
AGE: 52
SEX: Female
PERSONALITY: Expert

PERSONAL DESCRIPTION

Shoulder-length, curly blonde hair turning to grey, and a broad face that makes her look slightly fat despite her lean build. Gysbers has a calm, almost deferential manner that masks her intelligence and capacity for ruthlessness.

BACKGROUND

Gysbers was one of the first members of the OSS to be trained at Camp X in Ontario before the USA entered World War Two, and was trained by and worked alongside members of SOE, finally taking part in a number of covert missions in occupied Europe. It was then that Gysbers was recruited to Network N, and she has remained loyal to N and his mission through her subsequent service in the CIA. Gysbers has spent much of her career in Berlin. While she has been passed over as station chief on multiple occasions, as it is not seen as a suitable job for a woman, few people in the CIA know East Germany as well as she does.

IDEOLOGY/BELIEFS

Gysbers is a doubting Catholic who struggles with her faith in the context of the things she has seen and what she believes she has to do to keep her country and the world safe.

TRAITS

Fiercely loyal to those she considers friends; she is just none too sure who her friends are any more.

INITIAL MYTHOS EXPERIENCE

While studying cyphers at Camp X, Gysbers chanced upon a coded transmission intercepted in France that no one had been able to crack. She puzzled over it in her free time, almost as a hobby; it slowly dawned on her that the transmission was not encoded at all, but was simply in a language no one had recognised. In her attempts to understand the words, they began to infect her thoughts. Inhuman words crept into her speech, and her dreams were consumed by images of alien vistas and the endless spaces between the stars. One night she was brought out of a trance in the middle of some woodland near Lake Ontario by Percival St John, a British SOE trainer at Camp X; the forest was shifting around them in the darkness and it seemed like the trees themselves were walking. With the help of St John and N, Gysbers eventually returned to her senses, but she has retained a sensitivity to psychic emanations from inhuman sources.

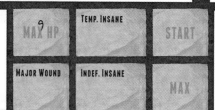

INVESTIGATOR

NAME Eleanor Gysbers
PLAYER _____ **PERSONALITY** Expert
OCCUPATION Intelligence Officer
SPECIALISM Intelligence Analyst
AGE 52 **SEX** Female
NATIONALITY American **AGENCY** CIA

CHARACTERISTICS

STR	50	25 / 10	DEX	50	25 / 10	INT IDEA	80	40 / 16
CON	40	20 / 8	APP	60	30 / 12	POW	70	35 / 14
SIZ	50	25 / 10	EDU	60	30 / 12	MOVE RATE	6	

HIT POINTS

Dying 0 1 2
Unconscious 3 4 5
6 7 8 (9) 10
11 12 13 14 15
16 17 18 19 20

MAX HP 9
TEMP. INSANE
MAJOR WOUND
INDEF. INSANE
START
MAX

SANITY

Insane 0 1 2 3 4 5 6 7 8 9 10 11 12 13 14
15 16 17 18 19 20 21 22 23 24 25 26 27 28 29 30 31
32 33 34 35 36 37 38 39 40 41 42 43 44 45 46 47 48
49 50 51 52 53 54 55 56 57 58 59 60 61 62 63 64 65
(66) 67 68 69 70 71 72 73 74 75 76 77 78 79 80 81 82
83 84 85 86 87 88 89 90 91 92 93 94 95 96 97 98 99

LUCK

Out of Luck 1 2 3 4 5 6 7 8 9 10 11 12 13 14 15
16 17 18 19 20 21 22 23 24 25 26 27 28 29 30 31 32 33 34 35 36
37 38 39 40 41 42 43 44 45 46 47 48 49 50 51 52 53 54 55 56 57
58 59 (60) 61 62 63 64 65 66 67 68 69 70 71 72 73 74 75 76 77 78
79 80 81 82 83 84 85 86 87 88 89 90 91 92 93 94 95 96 97 98 99

MAX MP 14

MAGIC POINTS

0 1 2 3 4
5 6 7 8 9
10 11 12 13 (14)
15 16 17 18 19
20 21 22 23 24

INVESTIGATOR SKILLS

Skill	%	/
◼ Accounting (10%)	40%	20 / 8
☐ Anthropology (01%)		
☐ Appraise (05%)		
☐ Archaeology (01%)		
☐ Art/Craft (05%)		
☐		
☐		
☐ Art/Craft (Forgery) (05%)		
☐ Artillery (01%)		
☐ Charm (15%)		
☐ Climb (20%)		
◼ Computer Use (05%)	21%	10 / 4
◼ Credit Rating (00%)	50%	25 / 10
◼ Cryptography (00%)	50%	25 / 10
◼ Cthulhu Mythos (00%)	2%	1 / 1
☐ Demolitions (00%)		
☐ Disguise (05%)		

Skill	%	/
☐ Dodge (Half DEX)	25%	12 / 5
☐ Drive Auto (20%)		
☐ Electrical Repair (10%)		
◼ Electronics (01%)	21%	10 / 4
☐ Fast Talk (05%)		
☐ Fighting (Brawl) (25%)		
☐		
☐		
◼ Firearms (Handgun) (20%)	40%	20 / 8
☐ Firearms (Rifle/ Shotgun) (25%)		
☐		
☐		
☐ First Aid (30%)		
☐ History (20%)		
☐ Intimidate (15%)		
☐ Jump (20%)		
◼ Language (German)	70%	35 / 14
◼ Language (Russian)	60%	30 / 12

Skill	%	/
☐ Language (Own) (EDU)		
◼ Law (05%)	25%	30 / 12
◼ Library Use (20%)	60%	30 / 12
☐ Listen (20%)		
☐ Locksmith (01%)		
☐		
☐ Mechanical Repair (10%)		
☐ Medicine (01%)		
☐ Military Science (00%)		
☐ Natural World (10%)		
☐ Navigate (10%)		
☐ Occult (05%)		
☐ Operate Heavy Machinery (01%)		
☐ Organisation (Soviet Knowledge (01%) Union)	60%	30 / 12
◼ Organisation Knowledge (Western Europe)	50%	25 / 10
◼ Organisation Knowledge (Eastern Europe)	70%	35 / 14
◼ Persuade (10%)	40%	20 / 8

Skill	%	/
☐ Pilot (01%)		
☐		
☐ Psychoanalysis (01%)		
☐ Psychology (10%)		
☐ Ride (05%)		
☐ Science (01%)		
☐		
◼ Signals (01%)	21%	10 / 4
☐ Sleight of Hand (10%)		
◼ Spot Hidden (25%)	45%	22 / 9
☐ Stealth (20%)		
☐ Survival (10%)		
☐		
☐ Swim (20%)		
☐ Throw (20%)		
☐ Track (10%)		
◼ Tradecraft (01%)	80%	40 / 8

WEAPONS

Weapon	Regular	Hard	Extreme	Damage	Range	Attacks	Ammo	Malf
Unarmed	25	12	5	1d3+db	-	1	-	-
Browning Hi Power 9mm pistol				1d10				

COMBAT

DAMAGE BONUS None

BUILD 0

DODGE 25

BACKSTORY

PERSONAL DESCRIPTION Shoulder-length, curly blonde hair turning to grey, and a broad face that makes her look slightly fat despite her lean build. Gysbers has a calm, almost deferential manner that masks her intelligence and capacity for ruthlessness.

WHY ARE YOU A SPY? Gysbers joined the OSS at its inception out of a sense of patriotism, and moved into the CIA after the war. She has been a spy for so long now that she can't remember any other life.

SIGNIFICANT PEOPLE Don Gysbers, her estranged husband. He didn't want to follow his wife's career around the world, and they separated. Still, whenever Gysbers travels back home, they always seem to end up in bed together.

MEANINGFUL LOCATIONS The site of the former US embassy in East Berlin, now nothing more than a ruin in the security zone. It is a symbol of everything that has gone wrong since the war.

TREASURED POSSESSIONS Her pet cat, Flowers, who is never quite as happy to see her as she would like.

TRAITS Fiercely loyal to those she considers friends; she is just none too sure who her friends are any more.

INJURIES AND SCARS

PHOBIAS AND MANIAS

ARCANE TOMES, SPELLS AND ARTEFACTS

ENCOUNTERS WITH STRANGE ENTITIES Gysbers attempted to translate a cipher of unknown provenance while working as a code breaker at Camp X, near Ontario, during World War Two. Her mind was infected with alien thoughts, leading to fugue states and strange visions. These recur in times of stress.

GEAR AND POSSESSIONS

Scanlock bug sweeper

CASH AND ASSETS

SPENDING LEVEL £100

STANDARD OF LIVING Wealthy

CASH £ 500 / P

ASSETS £50,000

(Note: Gysbers has assets mainly in US dollars and German marks, but they are presented in British pounds for consistency)

1 POUND (£) = 100 PENCE (P)

TRUST

AGENCY	%
CIA	40% (20/8)
Section 46	40% (20/8)

FELLOW INVESTIGATORS

Character:
Player:

Character:
Player:

Character:
Player:

ME

Character:
Player:

Character:
Player:

Character:
Player:

Character:
Player:

·INDEX·

WORLD WAR CTHULHU
THE DARKEST HOUR

The forces of fascism have overwhelmed Europe. Britain fights on desperately, and every man and woman must do what is necessary to avoid defeat.

In forgotten corners, darkness stirs. The cycles of the ancient god-things are measured in millennia, but those who serve them plot to take advantage of the chaos of conflict to advance their own schemes. For an unlucky few, the war collides with evils out of time, and they see and learn things that humanity is ill-prepared to encounter. The truly unlucky survive, and come to the attention of a certain spymaster, code letter N, who has plans for them. Pressed into the British espionage services, they are thrown into a desperate two-front war against the Axis forces and the insidious menace of the Cthulhu Mythos.

World War Cthulhu: The Darkest Hour is a World War Two core setting book for Call of Cthulhu from the award-winning team behind Cthulhu Britannica and The Laundry RPG.

· Details of British Intelligence organisations, what they did and the places they operated

· Customised Investigator creation rules with new wartime options, WWII game rules and equipment

· Keeper's guidance and information on Mythos wartime activities

· Investigator training guides on Intelligence work and Small Unit Tactics

· A complete campaign

CB71939
Price: $39.99
ISBN: 978-0-85744-179-9

CUBICLE 7 SEVEN

www.cubicle7.co.uk